MEN LOVE
THE SWEET POTATO QUEENS' BOOK OF LOVE, TOO

"Riotous, irreverent, and knockdown naughty—a must for any man who has ever loved a spirited woman, and for any woman who is one."
WILLIE MORRIS

"If everything in this book is true, I'm going duck hunting with a rake!"
KINKY FRIEDMAN

"*The Sweet Potato Queens' Book of Love* is hilarious and great. If Jill Conner Browne will say the magic words to me, I will kiss her right on the yam."
LARRY L. KING

"Funny and opinionated, *The Sweet Potato Queens' Book of Love* may be the hippest creation to come out of Mississippi since—well, since me, quite frankly. The Sweet Potato Queens themselves are rather buxom and single-minded. So move over, Monica Lewinsky! Who needs cigars when you have sweet potatoes?"
JOHN "LYPSINKA" EPPERSON

~ THE ~
Sweet Potato
Queens'
Book of Love

Jill Conner Browne

THREE RIVERS PRESS • NEW YORK

Published by Three Rivers Press, New York, New York.
Member of the Crown Publishing Group.

Random House, Inc. New York, Toronto, London, Sydney, Auckland
www.randomhouse.com

THREE RIVERS PRESS is a registered trademark and the Three Rivers Press colophon is a trademark of Random House, Inc.

Printed in the United States of America

Design by Lynne Amft

Library of Congress Cataloging-in-Publication Data
Browne, Jill Conner.
The Sweet Potato Queens' book of love / by Jill Conner Browne.—1st ed.
(pbk.)
I. Title.
PN6162.B735   1999
814'.54—dc21   98-41879
CIP

ISBN 0-609-80413-8

26   27   28   29   30

To
my daughter Bailey,
who is my very heart,
and
to the sweet memory of
Beth Griffin Jones,
who believed I could write a
really funny book

CONTENTS

Contents

~THE~

Sweet Potato Queens'

Book of Love

Meet the
Sweet Potato Queens

For anyone even remotely familiar with Jackson, Mississippi, the name "Sweet Potato Queens" instantly evokes sweet memories of beautiful, somewhat augmented female forms enveloped in green sequins, towering red hairdos, provocative dances, and the haunting refrain of "Tiny Bubbles," as only Don Ho could—or would, for that matter—deliver it. If, as they say, you ain't from around here, you need some enlightening; and your life will not be complete until you get it. Nor will it ever be the same after you do.

The Sweet Potato Queens are *us*. That would be me and eight or nine of my nearest and dearest. The Sweet Potato Queens were, however, my idea, and therefore I'm the boss of the whole enterprise. This is unquestionably the best job I ever had in my entire life.

It all began back in the early 1980s. Having passed recently through a pretty thick patch of doldrums, I was feeling a mite antsy and looking for a new direction for my life. My friend Cheri told me her dad had bought some land up the road a ways in Vardaman, Mississippi, which claims to be "The Sweet Potato Capital of the World." She said he had an old beat-up pickup truck on which he had meticulously painted ANGLIN SWEET POTATO FARMS. *Farms* may suggest to the reader an enormous spread, nothing but sweet potatoes as far as the eye can see. It was, in fact, twenty acres max—what he had was a fair-sized garden. The family thought it was pretty funny of him, and so did I. She went on to tell how Vardaman was into sweet potatoes in a big way, festival and all that. It occurred to me that they might need a Queen for that festival, and so I volunteered to be it on a continuing basis to save them the trouble and expense of selecting a new one every year. She said she'd pass along my generous offer to whoever might be interested.

Somehow that interest never materialized, but I had a passing thought that I might have stumbled on to something. The prospect of being the Queen of anything at all struck a chord deep within me. But I let it slide until I got a phone call from my buddy Viv. (I was lolling about in the bathtub—all the Queens love to loll about, in bathtubs and elsewhere; it makes us no never mind.) Anyway, I was in the tub lolling, and Viv called up to say that her husband, Malcolm, was going to put on a St. Patrick's Day parade. With literally no hesitation, I spoke the words that would forever change our worlds—I truly believe it was probably some sort of divine thing.

"I'm in it," I said emphatically.

"What are you going to be?" Viv asked, in a tone of mild disdain, as if I couldn't possibly have a plan already.

"I am the Sweet Potato Queen."

"Well, so am I," she said.

I said, "Fine." And it was done.

That first year, 1982, was a confusing one for the 350,000 residents of Jackson, Mississippi. The parade was held on the actual Day of St. Patrick, which happened to be a Thursday, I think. We paraded through downtown Jackson, right at five o'clock, so that all the folks getting off work could see us and be held up in traffic a little while longer. *Were they happy.* Prior to that very moment, St. Patrick's Day had passed virtually unnoticed in Jackson. It took us a few years to get the participation of our indigenous folk, but they are quite taken with the idea now.

So Malcolm White has his parade, officially called "Mal's St. Paddy's Day Parade," every year, now always on a Saturday in the general vicinity of the actual Day of St. Patrick—sometimes before, sometimes after, but always in March, I can promise you that. Other cities, I understand, are sticklers for March 17, but we, in our Southern way, are more concerned with the convenience afforded by a Saturday parade. I can't tell you what criteria are used to determine which Saturday. The only criterion that I'm personally aware of is that the Sweet Potato Queens will be the focal point. That has never been a problem.

The newly crowned Sweet Potato Queens were the instant darlings of that first parade. Our first outfits, however, were not nearly so grand as the ones we wear today. There were four of us, and we all wore green ball gowns from family trunks or the Goodwill thrift shop. And tiaras. God, I love a tiara. Suzanne Sugarbaker of *Designing Women* was so right when she said, "There's just nothing better in life than to ride around on the back of a convertible with a crown on your head." Words to live by. We didn't actually have a convertible; we had a pickup truck. But we did have big dresses, tiaras, and long gloves. (Our first gloves were the no-longer-quite-so-white ones we found in our mothers' forgotten wardrobes. Vivid colors would come in future years.)

And we had The Wave. That beauty queen wave, the Miss America wave—back when Miss America meant something; namely, that you were the best-looking thing in the whole country and none of this ridiculous scholarship hooey. Look at the old films of the Miss America pageant. The wave changed when they started all that scholarship crap. Scholarship, my butt. Take the crown out of the deal, and see how many contenders you got left. Name me any other *scholarship* competition in the universe that induces full-grown women to have their back teeth pulled, bottom ribs removed, noses whacked, and tits—well, brains will just never reach that level of popularity, now will they? Show me another scholarship contest that necessitates the application of Firm-Grip to one's buttocks to hold one's swimsuit in place. That's so all those brains don't pop out on the runway, no doubt.

Call the thing a beauty pageant, and be done with it. Get honest. And let the winners get back to the traditional wave, the one that says, *"I am better looking than every last one of you! But I am humble about it, and I have compassion for all you little, ugly, pathetic people. I am up here, where I belong, above the crowd, so you can all see how very beee-yooo-ti-ful I am and you can see it from all angles and so fully appreciate just how much better looking I am than you. But even in my great beauty, I am still sweet and kind, and I will wave to the likes of you to prove it. See? I am waving and smiling."*

And, with her arm nearly fully extended, she ever so gently moves just her hand, back and forth, back and forth, scarcely disturbing the air, the movement is so gentle. That's how Sweet Potato Queens wave. And I, being the Boss of Everything, am the only one who can claim ambidextrous waving skills.

So we're in this very first St. Paddy's Day parade in downtown Jackson, sitting up in the back of a green pickup truck with hand-lettered posterboard signs duct-taped to the sides proclaiming us to be the Sweet Potato Queens, riding up through some totally puzzled office workers. We just smiled and waved like we were *gen-u-wine* beauty queens, taking the whole thing very seriously, as if they should be so excited they got to see us, in person and all. And every now and then, in the tradition of Mardi Gras, we'd throw a little something to the crowds, only our throws, in keeping with who we claimed to be, were actual sweet potatoes, which are not usually as light-weight as, say, your beads or your doubloons. A sweet potato has a little heft to it, and it is fairly dense as well. Not quite the same as chunking bricks, but then actually pretty close to chunking bricks. One of the original Queens was quite the softball player, some kind of championship softball player. She could really hum them taters, let me tell you. I guess their size and odd shapes sort of affected her aim a little, since she lobbed one and nearly broke out a second-story window in the IRS building. We had to rein her in after that.

There was some initial confusion about our name. Sweet Potato Queens. Did the name describe the type of potato that we claimed to be the Queens of? Or were we the Queens of regular potatoes—Irish potatoes, maybe—possessed of good dispositions? It doesn't really matter to us. The Queen part is the only thing we care about at all.

We all knew we had what we needed to declare ourselves

Queens of whatever we chose. No pageants for us. No way would *we* ever consider groveling and posturing for a bunch of strangers, in full view of a live audience, in the pitiful hope that, for reasons of their own, they would decide to give us their paltry crown. Need I point out that not only are those crowns arbitrarily awarded, there's a very tight time constraint issued at the crowning. You get that crown for one year and one year only, sweetie, and during that year, you will step and fetch at the total whim of the folks who gave it to you. You do this for one entire year, at the end of which you are no longer Queen of Anything. You are a *former Queen*. Consider, too, the status of the other pathetic ninety-nine percent who entered the fray—losers, one and all, and no doubt scarred for life by the experience. Sweet Potato Queens, on the other hand, don't have to do jackshit that anybody says, and we are Queens for Life.

And another thing: Youth is not a prerequisite to becoming a Queen. The very young can have no sense of who they are, whereas the Sweet Potato Queens have had plenty of time to cultivate this vital self-awareness. Collectively we've had approximately four hundred years to devote to our development. And we've turned out rather well, I must say. We are a marvelously diverse lot. We have not one but two former presidents of the Junior League (we knew this about them and we still embraced them as if they were normal). We could see that they had learned painfully the folly of working one's ass off for an organization that didn't provide its leadership with even the hope of a crown.

Of course, as we know, Junior League work, grueling as it is, is free labor performed in one's spare time. The Queens all have real jobs as well. We have a former district attorney (no crown for that either), a commercial real estate agent, an interior designer, and an artist. One of us owns a gourmet kitchen store and sits on the board of about a half-dozen other businesses. One Queen designs and manufactures a line of women's silk and cashmere clothing and sells it at hotsy-totsy shops all over the country. We have an exercise and fitness consultant, and one of our number even owns a funeral home.

What I'm saying here is that the Sweet Potato Queens are real live grown-up women—self-sufficient and self-actualized. But we were crownless, one and all. Who, I ask, would be more worthy and capable of wearing a crown—the women I've just described or some eighteen-year-old surgically altered twit whose sole accomplishment is finally learning all the words to "My Way"? Who indeed. We consulted our mirrors and each other, and we could see pretty damn quick that we had It— that quality, that *je ne sais quoi*, that royal air that set us apart.

For the first few years, we were a democratic lot. Basically, anybody who had balls enough to put on a green ball gown from Goodwill and a tiara and perch on the back of a pickup truck, wave, and throw sweet potatoes was welcome to join the ranks of the Sweet Potato Queens. There were not as many takers as you might imagine. There's a whole passel of folks in this world who are content just to *spectate*, and to them we say, "God love you!" because we do so love an audience, and the bigger, the better.

But then came the Year of the Outfits. I was seized with a new inspiration—a vision, if you will—for the Sweet Potato Queens. I must confess that the source of my divination was the dance troupe for a small, historically black college in Mississippi—the Golden Girls of Alcorn State University. These incredible women perform on the field at halftime for the Alcorn Braves football games. They wear matching gold-sequined swimsuit-style outfits, and their dance routines are heart-stopping. They are my idols.

I have often said that it was merely an accident of birth that prevented my being a Golden Girl. They are all black, and I, sadly, am not. It's a bitch, but there you are. Live with it, I say. I also say that in my considered opinion white people were a mistake, on God's part, I mean. If He had it to do over, I bet he'd make everybody black, or at the very least see that the melanin got distributed a little more fairly. Face it, everybody would be better looking black. Any white girl who's ever had a tan can vouch for it. Especially if you have, shall we say, figure flaws? Brown fat just does not look as bad as white fat. Hell, you can tell that by looking at a pork chop. A strip of fat around a raw pork chop is all white and globby looking. Fry that sucker, and the fat comes out all crispy and golden brown.

Anyway, forced to accept that my own whiteness and also my age were going to preclude me from ever becoming a Golden Girl, I saw a way to make my dream happen anyway. The Sweet Potato Queens would fashion our costumes after those of the Golden Girls, only ours would be St. Patrick's Day *green* sequins instead of gold. And as long as I was designing the thing, why not throw in a little figure-enhancement? And so I went to my sister-in-law, Beth, who could tailor men's suits if she wanted to—she just doesn't want to—and explained my concept to her. She indicated that this would be "no problem at all." (She probably didn't really want to do this either, but I can be persuasive, not to mention persistent.)

We bought a basic swimsuit pattern in about a size 24, sort of one-size-fits-all, you know? She made the basic size 24 suit, stuffed the top and the butt with enough batting to make fifteen good-sized teddy bears, and then took up the waistline to fit each Queen. Weighing about forty pounds apiece, these giant sequined outfits are architectural wonders. The result was mesmerizing.

We were true crowd pleasers in these suits, proving that it *is* possible to please everyone all the time. For white males, it is impossible to have tits that are too big, and for black males, you cannot get the butt big enough. At the same time, if your tits are big enough, white guys don't care how big your butt is; and if your butt's big enough, black guys don't care what's happening around front. (We know all this because the Sweet Potato Queens are multicultural and we've compared notes.)

As far as we can tell, we are the only female drag queens in existence. Gay men love us. It's entirely possible that we are gay men trapped in straight women's bodies. Our lesbian friends adore us, too, because, hey, we are WOMEN. When we made our appearance in our new outfits on parade day, the crowd was galvanized. All the men wanted us, and all the women wanted to *be* us.

Just imagine the Sweet Potato Queens in our flowing red wigs—so vital for hair-tossing, which coupled with pelvic thrusting is the mainstay of our performance—wearing our official lipstick, Revlon's Love That Pink, and our majorette boots. God, how we love our majorette boots. Women of a certain age—I need not name that age—will empathize with this at once. When we were growing up, the Sears Roebuck Christmas catalog featured a wide array of costumes—the Bride's Dress, the Cowgirl Outfit, the Nurse's Uniform, the Princess Gown, and *the Majorette Suit*. With it were some crappy little spats that were supposed to pass for boots, but you could order separately Real Live Majorette Boots. Out of all the Queens with our diverse backgrounds, not one ever got a pair of Real Live Majorette Boots, and not one had ever gotten over that bitter disappointment.

That is so much of what being a Sweet Potato Queen represents for us: correcting karma—seizing the moment, re-creating ourselves from the soles of our majorette boots to the very tip-top of our towering red wigs. Don't waste your precious life moping over the vacancies of your childhood. Hell, you're full grown now. If you don't have Real Live Majorette Boots at this stage in your life, it's your own goddamn fault. Quit whining about it and go get some!

You may wonder why there is no mention of crowns. That's because we no longer wear them. In the beginning we needed them, we thought, to establish our Queenliness. Now, we believe, to wear a tangible symbol of our intangible yet utterly pervasive air of royalty would be redundant. We *are* the Sweet Potato Queens, and everybody knows it. Symbols are superfluous. Besides, it's really hard to keep a crown fastened to that big red wig.

I've often heard it said about us, in our presence, as if we weren't there or were perhaps deaf: "They turn into someone else when they put those outfits on." This is usually said by some Queen's boyfriend or husband. In fact, nothing could be further from the truth. We are completely ourselves when we put those costumes on. The Sweet Potato Queens are at one with the universe in those outfits.

The news media were all over us in our new regalia. "How does one get to *be* a Sweet Potato Queen?" the tiny white-girl reporter asked breathlessly. "It's like this, honey," I told her, with more than a small degree of disdain, "either you *are* a

Meet the Sweet Potato Queens

Sweet Potato Queen, or you are *not*." She looked perplexed. I added, "*You* are *not*." Whining, she persisted, "Well, how did you get to be a Sweet Potato Queen?" "First of all, missy"—even more disdain here—"I am *the* Sweet Potato Queen, by divine right, and I have handpicked my court. No woman gets on this float but by me. And let me tell you—there is plenty of sucking up involved in the process."

Ever since we first trotted out those green-sequined costumes and our amazing red wigs, I've been besieged by women from all over the country, begging, pleading, offering bribes of all sorts—all dying for the chance to put on that green suit and be Queen for a Day. But it's too late, I tell them all, too late. They had their chance back in the days of thrift shop dresses, but it's gone. Now you have to wait for someone to die or move to Australia to open up a vacancy. One current Queen had to grovel in the very dirt for three full years, even after an opening became available. It was so much fun having her follow us around year after year, in desperate supplication, we sort of hated to give it up. Like all sororities, we find that half, maybe more, of the fun is in keeping others out. So much for the sweet part.

Queens serve at my pleasure alone, and don't they know it. The sucking up doesn't stop with induction. It is a lifetime process, teamed with blind obedience. I design the outfits, I select the hair color and style, I select the music and choreograph the dances. I have ultimate power, and I like it.

Lest I give anyone the erroneous impression that the Sweet Potato Queens are an insular, independent group, let me assure you—nothing could be further from the truth. There are many happy, helpful worker bees in our little hive. Their hard work and devotion make it possible for us to reign supreme and serene. For this we are truly grateful, and we try to show our gratitude constantly. Indeed, we fraternize with all of them quite freely every day of the year, save one. Here's a rundown of Team Sweet Potato Queens.

A small but dedicated band of Sweet Potato Queen Wannabes is allowed to follow our float each year. We even let them wear our old outfits and discarded wigs. They carry signs that clearly mark them as Wannabes, engaged in their sucking-up process. Whenever our float stops for us to dance provocatively for our adoring crowds, the Wannabes run and prostrate themselves in front of the float, bowing, scraping, and generally whipping up increased crowd frenzy for us, the actual Queens. The Wannabes understand that any and all attention they might possibly receive must at all times be totally derivative. They are only Something because we are Everything.

Did I mention that the Queens adhere strictly and joyfully to the principle of equal opportunity? Indeed, one of our most devoted, talented, and hardworking Wannabes is of the boy persuasion, and we are all pissed off because George's butt is cuter than ours. Nonetheless, we've voted him Most Versatile, Miss Congeniality, and Most Likely to Become a Queen, gender notwithstanding.

Meet the Sweet Potato Queens

The Wannabes are by no means our entire entourage. With us since the very early years has been Wilson Wong, who for parade day is transformed into another persona. What do you get when you take a six-foot two-inch Chinese guy with waist-length hair and put him in a gold lamé smoking jacket and rhinestone sunglasses? You get: Lance Romance, the Official Consort to the Queens. He's the only man who has been allowed to ride on the float in anything less than a subservient capacity. Make no mistake; he *is* a veritable slave, but he's a love slave. All I can say is his wife, Lynn, is an unusually tolerant woman.

The Queens are too busy dancing and prancing in the parade these days to be bothered throwing trinkets to the masses. So we have many unpaid but happy lackeys to do our throwing for us—mostly our children, who ride in the back of the pickup truck that pulls the float. These are the "Tater Tots." People are always asking when we are going to let the kids ride on the float with us. To this ridiculous question, the answer is always the same: "When they get old enough, they can build their own damn float. We are not doing this for our children." Any idiot knows when you perform with children or animals, you become invisible, and that is not part of our plan.

The ever-growing contingent of hopeful, helpful men in our employ is known as the "Spud Studs." To say we would be nothing without them is stretching it a bit, but we would certainly be unduly inconvenienced, which is nearly as bad. And so we really love our Spud Studs, the guys who step and fetch on our behalf each and every year before and during the parade. They not only help build the float and hook up the generator and the sound system; they are solely responsible for getting it to the parade—no small accomplishment since this involves maneuvering a pickup truck towing a twenty-five-foot trailer bearing a fourteen-foot sweet potato down the interstate highway at three miles per hour with 250 pissed-off truckers backed up behind them for about thirty miles. The Spud Studs labor tirelessly on our behalf, literally for nothing, since most of them aren't even married to us anymore.

We could never perform without the atmosphere of safety provided by our vigilant Sweet Potato Queens Security Staff, those dedicated men and women who walk the entire arduous route alongside our float. Armed with Nerf bats, giant loofahs, and enormous loaves of rock-hard French bread, SPQ Security makes sure that the 65,000 slobbering fans who turn out to see us each year stay respectfully behind the police barricade. The officers of the staff—Meg, Michelle, and Rhonda—are so fetching in their little uniforms, a great deal of their time is spent defending their own honor as well.

The parade lines up on State Street, one of Jackson's main north-south thoroughfares, which you can get on and drive forever, and it will eventually take you to Chicago. We like for our float to be in about the middle of the lineup so the crowd has time to anticipate our appearance. This also puts us in position to spend a couple of hours before the parade begins looking at ourselves in the big picture windows at Lefleur's Cadillac. We like to arrive a good while before parade time to practice dancing on the float and to get accustomed to the pitch and roll of the contrivance. The float is a single-axle trailer, and that one axle makes all the difference. The float bounces around so much that dancing on it is not unlike surfing. You've got to get your sea legs early on to keep from landing out amongst the hoi polloi.

When the parade begins to roll, usually one-ish in the afternoon, we move past the sea of screaming people on State Street and turn down Capitol Street, the city's main downtown street, toward St. Andrews' Episcopal Cathedral. This is where one of the Queen's bosoms once leaped completely out of her costume and flung themselves at our friend Jerry McBride. Every year since, he has posted himself in the exact same spot but, alas, to no avail. Directly across the street from this seamy scene is the Governor's Mansion ("second oldest executive residence in the country after the White House," they say). The entire parade stops here while we work our magic on the parade judges, aka the Bucket Heads, so called because of their inexplicable fondness for wearing actual buckets on their heads. We always perform at least two dances here—one will be the theme song for that particular year, and the other is the perennial crowd favorite, "Who Wrote the Book of Love?" (Lots of pelvic thrusting in that one.) The governor himself usually comes out on his front portico to gape, and several members of the O'Tux Society will be there to curry our favor. A marching *krewe* (that's Mardi Gras lingo for "crew") of guys wearing green derbies and tuxedos with short pants, the O'Tuxers operate the flowers-for-kisses concession along the parade route. Bad boys all, at least on St. Paddy's Day.

Postperformance, we drive slowly away, leaving them all—governor, Bucket Heads, O'Tuxers, and crowd—in a state of utter satiety, and make our way down the remaining mile or so of the parade route, ending at Hal & Mal's for the street dance. Hal & Mal's, a popular Jackson watering hole owned by parade daddy Malcolm White, his Sweet Potato Queen wife, Viv, and his brother Hal, is the headquarters for the parade and quite naturally the official bar and eatery of the Sweet Potato Queens. (Hal & Mal's also has the best rest rooms in town. The men's room, our personal favorite, is a shrine to Elvis, with tributes to Elvis from famous people written on the walls, such as Billy Graham—"I think I will see Elvis Presley in Heaven." The urinals are made up to look like the front end of motorcycles.)

The Queens will make numerous appearances onstage with each band. We love all of the bands, of course, especially Raphael Semmes's local group, These Days, with lead singer Jewel Bass, but we're not shy about performing with the national acts; and Delbert McClinton is our favorite. (The greatest radio talk show guy of all time, Don Imus, loves Delbert almost as much as we do; somebody once said that Imus thinks the sun shines out of Delbert McClinton's butt, and we certainly have no evidence to the contrary.) The bands love us, too, because we can whip the crowd into a frenzy, and musicians do love a frenzied crowd. The end of the parade always comes too soon for us. Performing onstage at the street dance provides us our much-needed additional time to revel in our Queenliness.

In this rarefied atmosphere of Queendom, a philosophy, a way of life, has developed over the years. We've made many observations about life from our lofty vantage point above the masses—words to live by, axioms, and even laws that have been carved in stone. Finally we have decided to share them. *The Sweet Potato Queens' Book of Love* contains Everything You Need to Know About Life and Love. Life *is* Love. The Queens are always in love, be it with the Guy du Jour or a Hal's shrimp po-boy. It all feels good, and that is what's important.

So now, whenever the song raises the age-old question "Oh, I wonder, wonder who [ba-doo-doo], who [boom], who wrote the book of love?" you will know the answer: We did.

On the pretext of maintaining some small degree of anonymity, at least outside our own community, where we are all too well known, the Queens held a meeting and decided that we would all select stage names for use in this book. Everyone wrote down her first choice on a slip of paper and submitted it to me for approval. Well, wouldn't you just know it, everybody wanted to be "Tammy." We decided, quite rightly, I think, that it would not be fair to allow any one Queen to have the name that all wanted. And so we did the only fair thing: We will all be called "Tammy" henceforth.

That Queenly Look

MAINTAINING IT IN THIS LIFETIME AND THE NEXT

Getting and keeping that Queenly Look is no small feat, and you'd be amazed at all the details to which we must constantly attend. A good portion of our lives is, of necessity, devoted to our hair, our skin tone, our figure flaws, and our clothes. On parade day, none of this is a problem: We all wear huge matching wigs, we get tan enough (if only by the bottle or the bed) to avoid causing snow blindness in our audience, and in our fantastically enhanced matching outfits, our true body shape can't be discerned. But alas, we parade only one day a year, while we are Queens for Life, twenty-four hours a day, seven days a week. Certain considerations must be taken.

When the Wigs Come Off

The Queens are split about fifty-fifty, I'd say, in the hair department. What I mean is that half of us have some—as in lots, abundant, tons—and the rest of us have about four hairs each that we try in vain to frump and twitter into the semblance of Big Hair. Big Hair is highly desirable. You must have Big Hair to perform hair-tossing and -fluffing. This is the main activity of women in bars, and it is done not only to attract men but to intimidate other women. Because, trust me, other women are intimidated—especially if they happen to be other women to whom the hair gods were unkind. A thin, mousy mop cowers beside a Crowning Glory.

A friend of ours, Gail Pittman—an aspiring Queen who thinks she can ascend directly to the throne, bypassing the Wannabes—is a hugely successful, self-made businesswoman. She used to be a schoolteacher and now she owns and runs a gabillion-dollar company that produces her signature line of pottery and sells it in the finest shops nationwide. She has done it—made it. And in addition, she's the sweetest thing ever to draw breath. It would take a really small person to begrudge her the smashing success she has truly earned. You cannot help but love her at first sight. But sadly there are really small people in this world, and they are just the type who can only feel bigger if they make you feel smaller.

Gail was scheduled to make an appearance on a midsize town's local television talk show, and she had gotten all dolled up for the occasion, as she is wont to do: look nice for the people. For all her success and her universally renowned sweet disposition, our Gail does have a flaw; and she had the great misfortune of being in the clutches of one of those really small people, who also happened to be the local female talk show host. As the guy backstage was counting off the seconds-to-air time for them, *"Two...one,"* the host leaned over to Gail and said, "I thought so—you have thin hair! *You're on!"*

To say that Gail was undone does not even begin to describe it. She could hardly speak. She couldn't even think about what the creature was asking, for worrying about her hair and how very thin it must appear with all those lights shining through it and how she wished she'd worn a big hat. It was the longest ten or fifteen minutes of her entire life, and she has never fully recovered from it. We can only assume that this was the desired effect. I mean, what positive intent could be attributed to a woman who would say to another woman, immediately before a live television broadcast, "You have thin hair"?

Women with Big Hair talk with it the way Italians use their hands. They send messages with it and use it for punctuation. Their heads swivel like owls'. Women with Not Much Hair do not whip their heads about in the violent manner espoused by women with Big Hair. When desiring to look at something on the opposite side of the room from where we are currently gazing, those of us without Big Hair make a single, simple, discreet movement, one that does not disarrange our hair nor create strong wind currents that could endanger others. A Big Haired Woman, on the other hand, making the same turn will first duck her chin, then abruptly jerk it up and around, causing her massive mane to be lifted up and out in an alarming fashion, actually standing, for a moment, straight out from her head before collapsing and swirling about her head and face. Consequences to others depend on the length of said hair and the position of the hair in relation to its surroundings. Innocent bystanders can suffer lacerated eyeballs if they are not alert. Busboys have had the entire contents of their trays swept crashing to the floor by proximity to an ill-timed hair toss. An event of this magnitude, however, wouldn't be classified as a mere toss; such a grand toss is used primarily to communicate a willingness to perform sexual acts. When property damage occurs, it is usually the result of an actual hair fling, used to indicate extreme displeasure or, in the vernacular, being "pissed-off big time."

Some of the most energetic hair-flinging occurs in weight rooms. Remember that very first fitness show on TV—*The 20-Minute Workout*? It consisted, as I recall, of nearly naked women with huge hair contorting their bodies in unlikely positions and flinging their hair for twenty minutes. I don't know a single person who ever actually tried to do any of the supposed exercises. It was, however, a wildly popular show with the male demographic. The show is long gone, but hair-flinging as exercise has remained a constant in gyms all over the world. It caught on with Big Haired Women (BHW) everywhere.

The woman with normal to nominal hair, on the other hand, will simply lie down on the exercise bench, giving no attention whatsoever to the position of her hair. For her big-haired counterpart, the hair is the most important aspect and takes up most of the time. To perform, say, a leg curl, an exercise that requires one to lie facedown on a bench, the BHW, as she is lying down, will suddenly jerk her head back and then just as abruptly jerk her chin to her chest, causing all her hair to flip forward and hang off the end of the bench. No face will be visible for this exercise. Upon completion of the set, she will arise and fling it all back again. If she's performing the normal three sets of the exercise, the hair-fling will begin each and every set. If she chooses to remain on the bench in between sets, she will find it necessary to turn her head to face the other way from time to time. This is a very tricky maneuver for the BHW, requiring major head whippage in a horizontal position. Many cervical disks have been sacrificed in the perfection of this movement.

Big Hair can become a public menace. In locations where beauty pageants are big business, like Vicksburg, Mississippi, or the entire state of Texas, many establishments have taken precautions to protect their property and the safety of their non-BHW clientele. If you get too many women with Big Hair in one room, (a) there's not enough room for anybody else and (b) it gives the fire marshals fits because nobody can see the exit signs and somebody's sure to get trampled if a fire ever breaks out.

As a result, the Big Hair Hole was developed and patented by the owner of the F & M Patio Bar in New Orleans, Trevor Palmer. Touted as the most important Big Hair development since Aqua-Net, the Big Hair Hole is not only a safety device, it also insures that there will be ample space inside for even the most extravagant hair events. Upon arrival, Big Haired Women are directed to insert their heads into the Big Hair Hole to determine the exact size of their hair. This way, the maître d' can control the number of women with huge hair allowed inside at one sitting and can devise strategic placement as well. This provides a safe environment for participants and nonparticipants alike. In the event of a sellout crowd, latecomers are relegated to the Big Hair Holding Area until space is available.

The Unbearable Whiteness of Our Being

Several of the Queens—although, Lord knows, I love them dearly—are among those blighted individuals for whom the phrase "white people" was originally coined. *Zero* melanin in that skin, I'm saying. Freckles do not count. I, on the other hand, have been blessed with most of the melanin doled out to the white race in this hemisphere, and I'm plenty glad of it, too.

I'm also thrilled to report that my daughter got my skin and not that of her toad-belly father. When she was just a tyke, we had taken her to the beach, and she was naturally anxious to hit the sand. I cautioned her that we must wait and "grease up Dad—you know how he is." She looked thoughtful for a second and then said, "Yeah, he'll fry like a chicken in a rowboat." She was about two, and I have no idea where she came up with that analogy, let alone that perfect tone of disdain and disgust, but I've always preferred to think it was from her maternal gene pool.

Truly White People are understandably wild with envy regarding those of us with melanin-packed skin. One of the Queens, Tammy, and I had made a quick trip to Cancún to catch up on our lying down and lolling about. You don't want to get too far behind in those categories. Tammy, like most Truly Whites, had not the foggiest idea of how to get a tan; she desperately needed my expertise and assistance.

Now, in a tropical location such as the one we happened to find ourselves in, even bronze goddesses like myself must exercise a certain degree of caution about sunning. Let me just say right now that I'm well aware of all the current hoo-ha about the sun and all. And let me further state that I don't care what they say. The sun is good—for me. I believe that staying inside in fluorescent lights and working all the time is what is causing all this melanoma. I will add that I'm not a complete idiot and have no wish to look like my favorite pair of dark brown aged leather Bernardo sandals from high school. I wear 15 SPF all the time and still tan, and I love it. I will do it until I can no longer drag myself out of doors into a patch of sunlight. My theory is: Why not? We're all going to just wrinkle up and die one day anyway. If staying completely out of the sun for the rest of my life would make me look like I'm twenty-three when I'm sixty-five—I might consider it. *Might*. Na-a-ah. First, it can't happen, and second, what good would it do me to look like I'm twenty-three when I'm sixty-five? Who would I date? I have faced it: I am never going to be young and cute again, and I am over it. Let somebody else have a turn.

So Tammy wanted a tan. I knew I had my work cut out for me. We had to start the day early to handle it all. We'd go down and stake out our beach umbrella, watch the sun come up, have our breakfast poolside, and repair to the room to grease up. Tammy was stunned at the amount of preparation involved in proper tanning. Like most white people, she would typically fry herself totally the first day out and then spend the rest of her vacation in the room, watching TV standing up. She was uneducated in the proper application of sunscreen.

I explained to her, patiently, the absolute necessity of completely covering all of your flesh with lots of sunscreen and rubbing it in real good. Left to her own devices, she would have squirted a blob of sunscreen into her hand, rubbed her hands together twice, and then haphazardly smeared it on portions of assorted body parts. Some parts would have been devoid of any hope of protection, resulting in a sort of burned-in plaid or paisley design all over her body. I specified to her that any body parts she did not want crispy would have to be liberally coated with sunscreen. She was free to pick which ones she wanted to offer up to the sun god, but me, I was going to oil up *all* of my parts and go for a gentle sauté effect, leaving the deep-frying to the novices.

Tammy was also completely unaware that you are supposed to apply sunscreen twenty minutes before you actually need it, meaning you are supposed to let it soak in before you go out into the sun. Nobody reads labels. We greased up completely, no quick task given the amount of square footage we had to cover, and sat there dutifully, naked, for a full twenty minutes before suiting up and venturing out. I kept her to a rigorous schedule:

9–10 A.M.—reading under the umbrella
10–11 A.M.—sunning, thirty minutes each side,
    with occasional dips in the ocean
11 A.M.–noon—reading under the umbrella
noon—lunch, poolside
1–2 P.M.—nap under the umbrella

2–3 P.M.—repeat sun cycle

3–4 P.M.—repeat umbrella cycle

4 P.M.—shower, moisturize, and nap

Get up whenever, dress, and go out for dinner.

Repeat daily.j

Thanks to my expert personal tan management, Tammy did acquire a beautiful golden tan. We both developed coughs by the end of the trip, however, and we decided it was vacation pneumonia, caused by excessive lying down. We walk a fine line, don't you know, between a "therapeutic" dose and "overmedication."

How Does All That Look in the Mirror These Days?

From time to time the Queens have to make an assessment of the body situation. (Don't we all?) Unless you are Melissa Irby, our friend who grew to a flawless size two and stopped and has never added so much as a dollop of fat to her entire body—I hate her for it, we all hate her for it—I think we can safely say that this scene would best be played by candlelight. That reminds me of the guy who was going on about how his wife would never be "actually" unfaithful to him because she had had a whole bunch of kids and would never be emotionally secure enough to allow another man to see her body. I thought to myself, Now, I don't know everything; I'm just from south Jackson, after all. But down south of Raymond Road we have a little something we like to call the *dark*. He never considered the possibility that she might, if she found herself feeling frisky, just shoot out all the lightbulbs in the joint and roll around with the man of her choice until just before sunup the next day. All that is to say that the dark is our friend, and this is precisely what it was invented for. Most of us spend most of our time in the daylight, however, so it behooves us to get to the gym.

Once at the gym, you should hire a personal trainer who is knowledgeable about the two different types of muscles that make up the female body. You have your hiking-up muscles. They do just what the name implies: They hike up stuff that needs hiking up—your tits and your butt, for example. You should not need a breast reduction in order to make your waist smaller, if you catch my drift. Exercise the right muscles, and you can hike them babies back up where they belong. Then you have your pinning-down muscles; these are the ones you apply to other people. Proper use of your pinning-down muscles will assure that your man will stay right where you want him for as long as you want him there. Some muscles have dual purposes: They both hike up and pin down.

I said once that I thought a good goal for working out would be being able to Do It with the lights on. Our friend

Gail said her goal was to be able to try on swimsuits while wearing knee-highs. I don't believe there's a female body in existence, even size two Melissa's, that could stand up to that test without the aid of plastic surgeons, trick lighting, and computer enhancements. We have all struggled mightily with the exercise issue. We struggle to avoid having to do it as much as anything. We resist the idea. We wish it weren't so. If we exercise, however, we do look and feel much better in our outfits, not to mention how we look *out* of our outfits. And we've found we're happiest when we are not too fat to walk.

One of our Wannabes, JoAnne (see, you don't get to be a Tammy until you are an official Queen, and thus you enjoy none of the benefits of anonymity that are afforded the Royal Court), only recently started exercising. She has spent her entire life since shortly before puberty in the avid and relentless pursuit of nonathletic endeavors. If there was a world championship title for buttsitting, JoAnne would have been a contender. Until very recently she moved around only enough to avoid getting bedsores. The only thing that could possibly have incited JoAnne to exercise was the chance to be a Wannabe, with its attendant opportunity at being an *actual* Sweet Potato Queen, if she played her cards right.

She began exercising with a vengeance. From nothing to five and six days a week in a row. Walking, riding bikes, lifting weights, doing crunches. A maniac. Well, maniac could be a trifle strong—do maniacs whine as a general rule? If not, then

JoAnne would be disqualified, but she was, as they say, gettin' it with her neck out long and whining all the way. First her neck hurt, then her back had a twinge, then she was tired, then a knee started hurting—always something. But never enough to contraindicate exercise. Then she finally found what might be her ticket back to the couch: Her belly button hurt.

"Your belly button?" I asked, in a voice filled at once with incredulity and with disdain.

Those of us of a certain age were children in the time of the smallpox vaccination. You had to go to the doctor and get stuck a bunch of times on your arm. The resulting wound was expected to fester and ooze for weeks and then form a scab. And you had to be very careful of your scab; if it got knocked off before its time, you had to start all over again. Indeed, many's the kid that had to be dragged, under great protest, back to the doctor's office because the first vaccination didn't take. During that few weeks' time of incubating your vaccination, anytime something came up that you found distasteful or unpleasant, you immediately and loudly declared that you could not do *that* because it hurt your vaccination! You were bulletproof. It was the master key to the universe.

Even if parents weren't moved to pity by your pain and terror at having to be revaccinated, they were stirred to their core by the fact that you would not be allowed to enter the first grade without the requisite vaccination scar. Your starting school—and exiting the home—was vitally important to your parents, so having a freshly minted vaccination gave you pretty much carte blanche for what you would and would *not* be doing for the next few weeks. It was a heady experience of absolute power. It did not last forever, though many determined children tried to carry it on way past its time. A year later they would still be claiming alarming sensitivity in the vicinity of their vaccination.

For those of us of that generation, it has been a joke that has endured unto this very day; we can still try to weasel out of something by claiming that it hurts our vaccinations and, at the very least, count on a laugh from another *old* person. I knew a woman who would tell her exercise instructor she couldn't perform certain particularly unpleasant exercises because her eyes were dilated. She used this successfully for many years. Since the instructor knew that whenever the dilated eyes were invoked there was no future in trying to persuade Linda to do anything, she just acted sympathetic, to the amazement and disgust of the rest of the class.

Well, JoAnne may have hit on the ultimate hedge with the belly button business. If she does not, in fact, have one of those dreadful belly button hernias, which would be a tragedy and probably nip her exercise career right in the bud, she can still use it on a regular basis. Who can discern whether another person's belly button hurts? It cannot be proved or disproved, to my knowledge. We do have some leverage with her, however. There is a bylaw in the Sweet Potato Queens' Code of Conduct that prohibits being too fat to walk. If a Queen is too fat to walk, she's unable to fulfill one of her main functions, namely that of flouncing and prancing around on the float and through the crowds. She can't starve herself to achieve the desired size because she'd be too weak to perform her duties, and there's an even stronger prohibition against being skinny. Skinniness to even the slightest degree is not looked on kindly by the court. Indeed, it is simply not tolerated. No, Missy JoAnne is going to be forced to continue exercising, and we're so glad because she shows real potential. We are definitely grooming her for royalty.

She Who Laughs Last Laughs Best

The Queens do want to maintain their queenly look to the end. Another reason to get and stay fit is to try to live longer. One of the principal reasons this is such a deal, especially in the South, is that the longer you live, the longer you avoid having a typically terrible Southern obituary written about yourself. Perhaps this is not just a Southern custom, but we have certainly distilled and refined it. The first thing I read in the paper every morning is the lead obituary, which is the only one featuring comments from the grieving survivors. For many of the deceased, one could safely assume this is the only time their names have been in the newspaper. One would expect that those closest to the deceased would try to make this especially meaningful.

Here are some actual samples from real obituaries in legitimate newspapers. Honest to God. After reading them, you might want to take a moment and jot down a few notes for whoever will most likely be calling in your obit — just to be on the safe side.

He was fond of bowling and squirrels.

He enjoyed watching videos, *Matlock*, and *Wheel of Fortune* and eating candy.

She painted in oils—out of her head. She made up scenes, and she painted a lot of horses. She could make a horse look like he could talk to you. She especially enjoyed horses because her oldest granddaughter participates in high school rodeos and was named state reserve champion in the goat-tying competition.

"John" and his wife Ada Ruth have been bedridden for years but the family has continued to care for his cows.

I can never, never say what she meant to me. She was a true Christian who believed that Christianity was something you should not play with.

She never missed *Days of Our Lives* and had lunch ready to watch the stories every time.

"Sam" and his wife enjoyed raising St. Bernards. "We raised them and sold them. We sold them in about seven states in the South. They're just like most dogs. If you want them to be inside dogs, you keep them inside. Any you want to be outside dogs, you keep them outside."

She married at age thirty-three because she had been caring for her little brother who fell out of a tree when he was small.

Or they print revealing nicknames, such as "David 'Do-Nasty' Williams." But what follows is the world *champeen* obituary of all time. I will not be able to resist some commentary during the text.

Cause of death is undetermined pending the outcome of a coroner's investigation. "Betty Jo" was a friend that "Lou Ann" said she will never forget. "We have shared so many good times and there were so many things she did that turned many of our times into pure fun times." "Lou Ann" said that the deceased enjoyed cooking so much that she would cook in large portions—regardless of how many guests she would actually have. "I looked at the stove Sunday when I was at her house and I noticed what she had cooked. I honestly thought she must have planned for the students at the high school to come over and eat with her. She enjoyed cooking and eating—she would not mind telling you that." [I inferred from this that the departed one did not do so in a size four dress.] She has always loved shoes, and she will be buried in a pair of beige leather pumps her daughter "Poochy" recently bought. I am sure that when she walks through the Golden Gates [has she gone to Heaven or San Francisco?] her shoes will be shining and she will be smiling. And since she was always particular about her hair and wore it in a banana clip a lot [I swear to God, it said that], I am going to do her hair and makeup. We decided to let her look like she is getting ready for a night out—she is going to be just beautiful. We are going to let her wear it down and pushed off her face a bit so the angels can see those pretty eyes of hers. [Are we to assume that she was buried with her eyes stretched and pinned wide open?]

The lessons in all this are many, but to recap the high points for you: Stay fit and live long and prosper, but write your own obituary now, while you can, just in case.

The horrors wrought by supposedly good friends and close family members in the writing of obituaries give us food for thought on a related subject: burial clothes. If your "best" friend is going to put your hair in a banana clip while you lie helpless in your coffin and then tell the world about it in the newspaper, for crying out loud, what do you reckon the bitch will dress you in? She'll probably go out and buy you something since you probably don't own anything ugly enough to suit her. Whatever color you looked the worst in while living—you can only imagine how much worse you will look in it dead.

One of my favorite Wannabe Wannabes, Gayle Christopher, is a really pretty woman. (The Wannabes have gotten so snotty, they won't let any new ones join, so we have a whole crop of women sucking up to them now.) If you don't mention right off your own self how pretty she is, she will shortly find a way to work it into the conversation. If her best friend, Jean Hines, and I are trying to have a conversation that happens to have nothing whatsoever to do with how beautiful Gayle is, and Gayle is present, then every few minutes either Jean or I will have to glance at Gayle and say, right in the middle of our conversation, "Your hair looks great," or "That color is great on you." If we don't do this, she'll interrupt frequently with questions regarding her hair (doesn't it look great?) or her weight (doesn't it appear to be dropping rapidly?) or her nails (good color, yes?) or her general overall cuteness (I'm cuter than y'all are, right?), and so it's just easier to interrupt ourselves and give her what she wants. This woman has even pulled up beside us at a stoplight, rolled down her window, and hollered at us how she wished we could see her standing up because she had on the best-looking outfit and it looked especially cute on her. Then she punched her husband, John, in the arm and demanded, "Tell 'em how cute I look!" And just rode off, laughing, down the road. The thing is: She really is cute, and dang if part of what's so cute about her isn't how cute she says she is—unabashedly and loquaciously.

Gayle wants to leave this world looking just as cute. She has made us promise that we'll see to it that she's buried with clean and fluffy hair, with no gray showing, and wearing a pink negligee. Whenever she prepares to go out of town, she reminds us of our solemn oath concerning her burial preparations. We threaten to slap a gray granny-looking wig on her and dress her in a beige polyester double-knit pantsuit, two sizes too small so she looks fat, and with a high neck. The woman loves to cleave, if you know what I mean.

My sister, Judy, has always said that she would like to lie in state, propped up in her coffin with her eyes blared wide open, face fixed in a big grin, and have a taped greeting for all her mourners. Something real upbeat and, well, live-sounding, like:

"He-e-e-ey! Cuteshoestellyoumamahi!"

That is the gist of most conversations in the state of Texas. In Mississippi, a lot of conversations go like this:

That Queenly Look

"He-e-e-ey! KewtshewsyewthenkOleMissgone-
weeun?"

(If you were born north of the Mason-Dixon line, you probably can't imagine what's being said. I suggest that you read
each line aloud several times, sounding out the syllables pho-
netically until the words register. This would be a good prep-
aratory exercise if you ever plan to visit the South.)

The previously mentioned Official Consort to the Sweet
Potato Queens, Lance Romance, is in everyday life Wilson
Wong, devoted son of Mrs. Wong. Wilson was born on the ship
en route to the States when his parents immigrated from
China right before the big Commie brouhaha. Mrs. Wong does
not speak English. For years the family owned the best Chinese restaurant in town, and occasionally we'd try to reach
Wilson there. If she happened to be there by herself, Mrs.
Wong would answer the phone, and if the caller was not Chinese, like us, it was just too bad. "Wong!" she would shout into
the phone, and that was it. She had said the only word she
knew that could be understood by anyone outside her village.

Mrs. Wong's health has been failing of late, and when
asked how she was doing, Wilson said, "Well, she has her ups
and downs, but she's already been through five sets of burial
clothes, so we don't know what to think." He explained that it
is customary in China for a person to select his/her own burial clothes, obviously in advance of the actual day of burial.
But tradition says they can't be new clothes, so you have to

wear them at least once. Well, she keeps buying burial outfits and wearing them once, only to discover that she likes the outfit and keeps on wearing it. Then it ceases to be the burial outfit—apparently it can't be old clothes either—and so she has to start over. Since she cannot and will not die without proper burial clothes, we figure, at this rate she'll live forever.

The Queens had a planning session on the subject of burial clothes. The consensus was that no new outfits need be purchased, no funeral plans or cemetery plots arranged. We think that one fine St. Patrick's Day, right at the end of the parade, we will all just ascend, in full regalia, right off the float and directly up to Heaven. It seems the only plausible ending to us, and it is the only one we could all agree on.

2

The True Magic Words

GUARANTEED TO GET ANY MAN
TO DO YOUR BIDDING

Given that it's not easy, painless, or inexpensive to be a Sweet Potato Queen, that tells you right off that outside assistance will be required. We postulate that this is true whether one is a Queen or not. We feel that in any area of life, it is highly desirable to get other people—men—to do things for you whenever possible. This includes, but is certainly not restricted to, performing all manner of personal services, as in cooking, cleaning, and errand-running, and especially rubbing, fawning, worshiping in word and deed, constantly, and of course, paying for things—as in everything, including, naturally, presents of all kinds, but especially the sparkly kind. We find that we are very crowlike in our affinity for things that go sparkle.

Toward this end we have formulated the True Magic Words. Let me assure you, these words used correctly just beat the hell out of *please*. As a matter of fact, if you use these words aptly, you can forget the word *please* even exists—except that you will be hearing it spoken to *you* so much, you will come to gag on it. With these simple words you will have the instant ability to persuade any man on earth to willingly, happily, and swiftly do your bidding. This is one hundred percent guaranteed. The Sweet Potato Queens, as a group, have employed this technique for more than twelve years now, and we have an absolute no-fail rate thus far.

Here's what you do: First, decide what it is that you want or need done, handled, fetched, or purchased. Then select the man you want to perform this task. It doesn't matter which man. For the purposes being discussed, they are interchangeable. Anyway, pick a guy, any guy, and outline for him, in vivid detail, exactly what you will require of him. It is vital that you cover all the bases at this point in the discussion, because once he hears the words, he will be momentarily slack-jawed and breathless, and then his brain will irretrievably lock. He is a man with a mission, and he is going to do whatever you want so fast, your head will spin, so get out of the way.

The True Magic Words

So you've followed the steps so far. You've identified your want/need. You've selected the designated guy. You've shared with him in minute catalog your heart's desire. You are ready for the Magic Words. The words have been uttered so successfully so many times in Jackson, Mississippi, and abroad by the Sweet Potato Queens that they have become known as the Sweet Potato Queens' Promise, or simply, the Promise. And what we do is this. One or more of us will visit the designated guy and make the pitch: "And if you will do this one little ole thing for us, we promise that"—and here's what clinches the whole deal, the True Magic Words—"we, all eight of us, will give you a blow job."

And then we shut up.

A traditional moment of silence is always observed immediately following the use of the Magic Words. Men are inherently slow regarding women, and the moment of silence allows for lag time. Men's brains are migratory and are usually located in their summer home, way south. The silence of the moment is palpable, just like those few seconds before the sun slips into the ocean. The man is transported. When breathing is restored, it is almost always mouth breathing.

Do not, under any circumstances, utter another word after the True Magic Words have been spoken. Any sales manual will tell you that, once you have made your offer, the next one who speaks loses. And trust me, ladies, he will speak. Okay, maybe he won't actually speak. There may not be time. He may have just launched himself out the nearest window in his rush to comply with your wishes. But the result is the same. With these few Magic Words, you will be able to persuade any man on earth to swiftly and happily perform any and all requests you make.

And now, let me hasten to explain to you, as you will to him: *There is a vast difference between the promise of something and the receipt thereof.* What he has received is the *Promise.* But it's no trouble at all to help him see that, even with only the Promise, he is miles ahead of where he was without it. He is actually in the ballpark now. It could happen. It won't, never has, but it doesn't matter. Men just love to hear you say the words.

Talk about shooting fish in a barrel. This is so easy. If it didn't make them so happy, we'd probably feel bad about it and quit. And it works so damn well! I'm telling you, we've used this technique repeatedly throughout the civilized world, very often with the same men. Not only have we never failed to get what we want, but to date not one Promise has ever been fulfilled.

The giving of the Promise has become the Sweet Potato Queens' rite of initiation. Once a woman has been selected for a position in the court, the Boss Queen, namely me, will choose a quest and a knight for her to practice on. The entire court will accompany her on her virgin mission. It is a very moving occasion.

The True Magic Words

A few years ago, at the initiation of Tammy, which was being held during happy hour at Hal & Mal's, we spied at the bar a certain high muckety-muck from the *Clarion-Ledger,* the largest newspaper in Mississippi. And we—rather, I—decided that it would be a good thing if he would ensure that there was a large, full-color, above-the-fold, front-page photo of the Sweet Potato Queens in Sunday's paper following the parade on Saturday. And so our newest Tammy went over to him, accompanied by the full court of Queens. Now he, not living under a rock, knew full well who we were, what we wanted, and what we were about to say to him in order to get it. So did everybody else at the bar, which, of course, did make him the Man of the Hour—lucky bastard. Still, not being accustomed to receiving such attention, he was slightly flustered and flushed. Meanwhile our girl Tammy, former president of the Junior League and former Queen Regent of the Girls' Auxiliary of the First Baptist Church of the little town where she grew up, was in an equal swivet at the prospect of actually delivering the Promise to this man, in full view and earshot of a hundred or so people, all of whom were respectfully silent in keeping with the import of the occasion.

All I can say is: I now have that large, full-color, above-the-fold, front-page photo framed and hanging in my office.

On another occasion a covey of Queens drove forty miles to Vicksburg because Jason D. Williams was playing outdoors on the banks of the Mississippi River, at a club over there, and the Queens were in a dancing mood. If you're in a dancing mood, Jason D. is a good man to help you out. He is a piano-playing fiend, that's what he is. He plays like Jerry Lee Lewis's wet dream. But on that night, Jason D. began positively crooning songs like "Bringing in the Sheaves," which is highly entertaining church fare but not what we had in mind for a Saturday night out of town. We made inquiries of the sound man about how long we could expect this to go on. He indicated there was just no telling what Jason D. might do or when he might do it. This was not acceptable. The Queens were in a froth to dance.

One of the Queens, possibly me, hastily scribbled a note on a cocktail napkin and marched herself through the thicket of chairs, up the steps, and across the stage and plunked the note down on the piano, right under the nose of Jason D., who was at that time right in the middle of a touching ballad. What the note said was this: "There are six of us who came over here to dance, and we will all give you a blow job if you will crank it up *right now!*" Well, I'll have you know that Jason D. kicked his piano stool off into the river and commenced flailing on that piano in a manner most exciting to the Queens. We flocked to the front and twirled and undulated to our own delight—and that of the band as well. As a result, we didn't have to pay admission to the second show, and we drank free, too.

Whenever possible, we like to make the Promise in a

group. It seems to heighten the excitement for the guy. We're all laughing fit to kill, and he knows on some level—like his conscious, rational mind—that it is never going to happen. But on some other level, usually a little farther south, hope springs eternal, and we are all for keeping hope alive, especially since it serves our purpose so well.

We are mindful, however, that a power this, well, *powerful* cannot and should not be used for our own purposes alone, no matter how worthwhile and important those purposes may be. No, we feel honor-bound on occasion to use this power for the good of others as well. Draw nigh and hear testimony of our touching concern for the health and well-being of our brother. A number of years ago, one of our dearest friends and biggest fans, Sergio Fernandez, was stricken with that weird temporary paralysis stuff, Guillain-Barré syndrome. This was not a handy disease for a keyboard-playing father of two to come down with. As it progressed, he became completely paralyzed, and he spent a good bit of time in a rehab hospital. Being universally adored, Sergio had everybody breaking his or her neck to help him out. Folks were praying for him and raising money. We felt that the Queens could do more. And so we did.

Me and one of the longest-serving Queens, Tammy, suited up in full Queen regalia and paid a hospital call. When we arrived on Sergio's floor, the nurse informed us that we would find him in the patients' lounge. We made quite an entrance, as you may well imagine. Sergio was, of course, elated to see us. He said our arrival had been duly noted from the windows of the lounge by some of his fellow patients, and no one had believed him when he wheeled over, looked out, and said nonchalantly, "I know those women." So imagine their awe and his triumph when we swept in and came immediately to his side.

We sat and chatted for a bit and inquired about his progress. He was proud to announce that bath time was a happy time and that the nurses were pretty good-natured about it. He was just so ecstatic to receive confirmation on a daily basis that *everything* was not paralyzed. We said we were happy to hear that, and that brought us to the real reason for our visit. "We have come to heal you, Sergio," we told him gravely. He seemed willing. And then we told him that if he would get well and quick, we promised that we would all give him a blow job. And so, of course, he did, and, of course, we didn't. But he has never complained.

This technique will work on any man, anywhere, anytime. There are certain words and/or gestures that are the same in any language—Mayday, visa, exit, okay, grabbing your throat to tell the world you are choking. You can no doubt think of other examples. Well, blow jobs are that way—timeless, universal, always desired and appreciated. Everybody wants a blow job all the time.

Women are not like this. As much as we love sex, there are times when we really and truly are not interested. One of those times would be, say, immediately after we have eaten an entire pizza. This is known as Whole Pizza syndrome. You know, you're stuffed to the gills, your stomach looks like you ate a basketball, whole and inflated; you're starting to get that comfy, sleepy feeling, and here he comes, pawing at you. He could not have been interested before you ate the entire pizza, when you were alert and had that flat stomach. No, he wasn't interested then because he was hungry, and he can think only about his overriding primal need at any given moment. Once he has eaten, peed, had a beer, put out the fire in his hair—satisfied whatever urgent need he happens to be having at the time—then his mind immediately reverts to the one subject it is totally consumed with 99.9 percent of his life, waking or sleeping: sex, or more precisely, blow jobs.

At any rate men could do a lot better—meaning, get what they want—if they would just pay attention. If their thoughts weren't totally focused on blow jobs all the time, they might be able to think clearly enough to formulate more successful strategies than suddenly grabbing some of our body parts and inquiring bluntly whether we wanted to give them one. How many times has this happened to you, and how many times have you responded with a resounding, "Yes, I was just thinking the whole time I was drinking that pitcher of beer and eating that thirty-six-inch fully loaded pizza, that as soon as I finish all this, I'm going to pounce on you like a duck on a June bug"?

You, at this point, having just consumed an entire pizza, would rather be set on fire than have sex with anybody, let alone anybody as stupid as he is to think that you'd be in the mood. This has happened after virtually every meal you've ever shared with him. Men are persevering little shits; you've got to give 'em that. They'll just keep right on trying. The puzzle is this: Why, when something doesn't work ever, do they keep trying the same thing? Why does it never occur to them to change strategies? Just once, why can't he figure out that everybody loves cold pizza *after* sex?

I dated a wonderful guy, Ralph, for an all-too-brief period in my youth. At the time he was totally unsuitable for me: tall, dark, handsome, sexy, successful, great sense of humor, sweet, smart, really fun to be with—you get the picture. There was no way I'd get serious with a guy like that. I preferred the unemployed, although the unemployable were particular favorites, too, in those days. But anyway, Ralph also happened to be Jewish. I am not, and he made constant witty references to this shortcoming on my part, referring to me as a "white woman." When he would say it, he would affect this really thick drawl and stretch it way out, with a very long, flat "eye" sound in "white." On one occasion he made the mistake of making an ill-timed pass; he was normally a brilliant tactician. Upon being rebuffed, he commented, "Ever'body knows, whi-I-ite wimmin don't li-I-ike to be pestered."

The True Magic Words

Yes, indeed. Blow jobs make the world go 'round, just in case you still thought it was love. Everything that happens, good or bad, in the entire world, can ultimately be traced back to a blow job, either given or withheld. Men have two states of mind that can be best illustrated with two crude drawings: one of a big, smiley, happy face; the other of a big old scowl. The accompanying captions would read "Blow Jobs" and "No Blow Jobs." Properly timed and executed, blow jobs given to the right personnel on a regular basis would no doubt bring world peace. Perhaps we should unleash all those beauty pageant contestants who are always clamoring to work for world peace. Put 'em out there where they can do us all some real good. Save the whales, the children, the rain forests, the oceans, the ozone layer, the owls, the beach mice—everything! Save 'em all! They've got to organize! A union is what they need.

But we know the secret truth: The Promise of a blow job works just as well as the real thing, at least from our perspective. We deduced this important principle from a tip I read some years ago in "Hints from Heloise." One clever mom had discovered how to avoid the sticky mess that always occurred when she gave her children ice cream. She swore they were just as happy with an *empty cone!* I recall thinking those must be some serious dumbass kids if they couldn't tell the difference between ice cream and no ice cream. Turns out she was 100 percent correct. And so it is with the utmost confidence that we recommend The Promise to you. According to Tammy, Queen and In-house Counsel, the Promise is not enforceable in any court of law. Believe me, if it were, with as many lawyers as we've used it on, we'd have heard about it by now!

3

The Best Advice
Ever Given

IN THE ENTIRE HISTORY
OF THE WORLD

For the most part Sweet Potato Queens prefer the *giving* of advice over the *taking* thereof, with a few notable exceptions. The following story from my childhood represents advice I am proud I was given. Naturally I want to pass it on to you. My father's people (in the South, your family is called your "people") were from a "suburb" of Kosciusko, Mississippi, called Ethel. Kosciusko is also Oprah Winfrey's hometown, but you're not likely to see her at the Piggly-Wiggly on a regular basis. The town did have a big deal honoring her some years back. I was prevented from attending by the advanced state of my pregnancy—that time that used to be called "the confinement," when you are just too huge to be seen by the unaided human eye and it requires a panoramic lens to take you all in. I have always regretted that I missed getting to see her in my daddy's hometown, since Oprah is one of the few celebrity types I really admire.

Other than Oprah (who is no longer there), woods and red dirt roads were, and still are, the dominant features of the area. This is not to say that those characteristics would differentiate Ethel from any of a jillion other little hamlets in the South. We mostly sort of lump them all together under a few generic names for the sake of shortening the telling of tales. "Podunk," "Bumfuck," and "East Jesus" cropping up in a story would indicate to you one of these places with not much else but woods and red dirt roads. Graveled roads in some of these vicinities are considered to be newfangled ideas. As are teeth.

But anyway, we went to see my grandfather in Ethel a lot when I was a kid. He was deaf as a post for as long as I can remember. I also remember that he didn't seem to mind in the slightest being deaf as a post. Most likely that was because he was a lot more interested in monologues than dialogues. We all referred to him as "Harvey" since he couldn't hear us say it. Seems he didn't like to be called that, and since the beginning of time my grandfather had told everybody his name was Philip. Harvey was, in fact, his name, but this did not become known until Daddy was a full-grown man and named his own son Philip after my grandfather. Only after the naming did my grandfather 'fess up that his true name was Harvey. This irritated Daddy to the extent that he refused to call the man anything but Harvey ever again. My uncle fell prey to the same ruse. Somewhere in Pennsylvania I have a cousin Philip who was named for his grandfather, Harvey. Normal family.

But then, maybe not quite as "normal" as some other families in the Attala County area where my people lived. There was one guy who was called by all who knew him "Hoe Handle"—only the *d* in Handle wasn't pronounced. It was "Hoe Hannel," or more often just "Hannel," on account of him stepping on a hoe once, probably forty-five years earlier, and whacking himself smartly between the eyes with the handle. He apparently never quite succeeded in living it down. Then there was this other guy who was universally addressed as "Big Dick." Even his own mother called him "Dick." This was unusual because his name was Charles or something. I can't imagine how that got started. So, all things considered, I guess the Philip/Harvey thing was pretty tame.

Granddaddy Harvey always wore the same thing: gray wool pants, black belt, white long-sleeved shirt buttoned to the neck, black hard-soled shoes, and gray felt hat. Winter or summer, it never varied. He was old, always old, and thin as a rail, with skin like parchment paper. He rolled his own cigarettes from a little cotton pouch he kept of Country Gentleman tobacco. He smoked the entire thing. There was no cigarette butt, ever, not even so much as what would be called a "roach" today. It was simply gone. Ecologically sound, I suppose, in a twisted sort of way. I once brought him some strawberry-flavored papers I'd bought at a head shop in Atlanta. He looked like a really old, skinny Jerry Garcia puffing on a joint. He could squat for days, his skinny little butt just grazing the ground. He would sit like that for hours watching me ride my horses in the lower pasture. When he got tired, he would simply rise. No groaning. No pushing with his hands. He would simply stand straight up and walk away. I did not inherit his knees.

When the time came for us to leave, he would walk us out to our car. "Us" being my parents, my older sister, and me. We would be getting into whatever model Ford Daddy was driving at the time—that is, until he got mad at Ford for something and started buying Buicks. He was like that. Totally brand loyal until the manufacturer did something he didn't like, and then he would quit them forever, never to reconcile. He quit Gillette and Falstaff and took up with Schick and Old Milwaukee the same way, just for spite.

My grandfather would walk us out to the car, and he would always say the same thing as we were leaving. He'd never use any of the usual ones, like "Be careful," "Be sweet," or "Be good." Mamma used all those on a rotating basis. Daddy's parting shot was always "Don't fuss with your mama." No, Harvey would wait for Daddy to roll down his window, and then he'd prop those skinny elbows on the ledge and stick his whole head, hat and all, in through the window. And he would say, "Y'all come when you can," which was of no substantial pith or import, but then he would add, "Be particular." Except he pronounced it "p'ticklar."

Be particular. That is, without a doubt, the Best Advice Ever Given in the History of the Entire World. Consider, if you will, the profound effect that following advice would have on, say, your diet, your love life, your financial situation, your decision on whether to have that next drink. I mean, what do those two words not cover?

The times when one has not heeded this sage advice will stand out with alarming clarity. Huge amounts of pain and money are frequently associated with such times. Just to show you how awry things can go when one is not particular, I offer this personal testimony from one of the Queens, Tammy. Whenever the subject of sexual escapades presents itself—and in a group of women it presents itself fairly often—Tammy always offers this as her most bizarre sexual experience to date.

The Redheaded Man Who Would Not Move

"Whenever I think of him to this day, some twenty years later," Tammy says, "I always think of him in capital letters—THE REDHEADED MAN WHO WOULD NOT MOVE.

"It was like this: I had been dating this guy for a couple of months. Somehow, don't ask me, it happened that I had been dating him all this time and hadn't gotten around to sleeping with him yet. Anyway, we had a relationship by this time that was based on stuff like friendship and companionship, and I really liked the guy a lot. So it got real weird, real quick once we Did It.

"This guy had the most bizarre approach that I have ever even heard of, let alone experienced. If there was any of what is commonly referred to as 'foreplay,' I totally missed it. I swear to this day, it never happened. The way I remember it, there was no activity between the time that we got our clothes all the way off and the time that he lowered his entire—and it was substantial—body weight onto me. There was no customary propping-up-on-the-elbows stuff—I got the full load. And there it remained, parked, dead still, motionless for what seemed like an eternity. During which time many probing questions entered my mind, as you may well imagine. Things like 'Huh?' Come to think of it, that was probably the only question that came to me at that particular time. But it got repeated over and over.

"Every time I tell this tale, somebody will ask me why I didn't just take over the situation. There are at least two answers to that question, which did occur to me at that time. The first one was that I was doing good—with all my effort— to maintain airflow to and from my lungs, squashed as I was. What most people, I think, would consider the 'normal' movements associated with the, ahhh, missionary position cannot, for the record, be generated solely by the party in the lower position without the full cooperation of the party in the upper position, if the party in the upper position outweighs the party in the lower position by a good seventy-five pounds. And this, I'm afraid, is the unhappy position in which I found myself, with no help in sight.

"The second thought that came to me was this: 'He obviously does not think that you are supposed to move during this procedure and thus would be shocked, horrified, if not outraged, by any attempt at movement on my part.' I imagined him saying to me, through gritted teeth, 'Ladies do not move!' And as I was in no position to argue the point, I let the moment pass without comment.

"But this, I am so sorry to report, was not the end of it. I rationalized the situation to death. I concocted I don't know how many 'reasons' to explain away the event, or nonevent, as it were. I guess, in retrospect, I must have come up with something satisfactory, because I fell for it—again. Yes, indeedy-do, a few nights later found me in the same predicament as before. Only this time it was much, much worse because I knew what could happen—or in this case, could not happen. And danged if it didn't. A repeat performance of the nonperformance.

"Well, let me tell you, it was a difficult situation I found myself in, and I knew if I allowed myself to think even one thought about it, it would be all over. I'd start laughing, and I'd never be able to stop. So I thought about dead dogs. It was the first thing that came to mind that was not funny, and I just honed in on it and thought about it as hard as I could. Until it was over.

"After that I told him I thought we ought to just be friends, and he moved away. All's well that ends well. No blood, no foul. No tickee, no washee. A rolling stone gathers no moss. I don't know what clichés would fit this particular situation best, but I do know, at the very least, I've never forgotten the Redheaded Man Who Would Not Move."

The moral of this story should come as no surprise: *Be particular!*

4

Be Prepared

ON ACCOUNT OF
YOU JUST NEVER KNOW

The first rule of being prepared is, of course, *always shave your legs*. In a perfect world we would not even have to mention armpits, but sadly, even in the rarefied atmosphere of the Sweet Potato Queens' domain, the hairy armpit issue has materialized. We have one Queen—she's the youngest, and she missed the whole hippie thing when it was original, and she's being forced to live through it now, when it is so over, since she chose to move to Boulder, Colorado, where it is apparently the height of chic to be an ugly woman. At any rate she has not grown up and out of it sufficiently yet to begin—or I guess *resume* would be more accurate—shaving her underarms, and so we have to do a pit check on her when she comes back to Jackson every year at parade time. (It should be duly noted that she's so beautiful and queenly that, even with hairy armpits, she's a knockout and thus has become a tourist attraction in Boulder.)

Shave everything that needs it, and by all means, *always wear pretty underwear, on account of you just never know.* I know your mother said you should always wear clean underwear, but at this stage of your life, you really should not need to be reminded of this one by anyone, including yourself. Clean is a definite given. And clean would be sufficient if the only unexpected aspiration you have is something along the lines of a car wreck. However, it would seem to me that if you've just had a head-on collision with a Peterbilt or a Mack truck, chances are excellent that the clean factor has been torn asunder anyway.

So let's look on the bright side of things and hope for something unexpected of the tall, dark, and handsome variety. The mood will be destroyed if you are wearing orthopedic underwear. It must be pretty. It must also be tiny. How many of James Bond's girlfriends have ever shown up in big underpants? Pretty and tiny are both readily available ready-made; however, the Queens do not like to buy off-the-rack. We prefer instead to travel to the West Coast, where we can camp out at our friend Ned Walton's house in the Hollywood Hills, which is the most serene spot on the planet and we wish we could live there all the time. From our campsite at Chez Ned, we can go to a little place on La Cienega called, aptly, Trashy Lingerie. Owned by the incomparable Miss Tracy, her helpmate, the ineffable Mitch, and their devoted son, Randy, Trashy Lingerie is a delightful little shop wherein they custommake—what else?—trashy lingerie. And I do mean custommake, too. In the course of your fitting, you will be measured in ways your dressmaker never dreamed of. Nipple to nipple. Cheek to cheek. But, hey, your underwear will fit.

A good fit in underwear is a definite advantage when you're wearing the pretty stuff—"single underwear" is what I call it—because otherwise it can be miserable. Bras crawl up your back or down your belly (if they're strapless). Slips ride up and stick to your dress. Straps fall down. And panties— Lord, deliver us from pretty panties. You just put them on, and they immediately wedge up your butt, you don't even have to move. Thongs were a perfectly natural progression—why not save all that extra material, they all end up in the same place anyway.

My friend Gayle, the one who's so good looking and not only knows it but tells us about it all the time, and her husband were in Florida for a romantic getaway. They had retired for the night, and he commenced fondling her loins in that way and commented, huskily, that he loved that new thong she was wearing, to which she snappily replied, "Oh, John! Don't get all excited; my panties are just up my crack!" Then they both laughed so loud, the people in the next condo complained to the management. Our Gayle can make a mood or break it just that fast, but it keeps ole John on his toes, let me tell you.

But answer me this—how come they don't make men's underwear so it goes up their butts, huh? Same thing with swimsuits. Even guys who wear those dreadful Speedos, they put 'em on and they stay put. The only women whose swimsuits don't crawl up their butts are the ones in beauty pageants, and that's only because they use Firm-Grip stuff on their butts. I call this unfair. I propose that they either make stuff for us that will stay down—or make all the men's stuff so it crawls up their butts. I don't care which—I'm just looking for parity here.

Actually, a good case can be made for "married underwear." "Married" may be a misnomer; it may be "postpartum underwear" I'm speaking of. Perhaps women who have never had children continue to wear beautiful underwear till the day they die. I'll have to verify that point. At any rate a big change occurs shortly after conception, and as far as I can tell, it is irreversible. For one thing they do not make pretty underwear for pregnant women. They make orthopedic underwear for pregnant women—big, sturdy, serviceable, substantial Russian immigrant underwear. And it's indescribably comfy. This means that, once you've experienced it, you may never go back.

This brings us to another essential principle of prepared-ness: *Never Wear Panties to a Party.* This rule evolved quite by accident when I was severely pregnant. My erstwhile husband, the ubiquitous MoonPie himself, came in the room where I was struggling to clothe my behemoth body for some festive occasion. I had somehow managed to stuff myself, sausagelike, into a very tight casing of maternity pantyhose. Those and one of those gigantic bras, the cups of which would fit on my head, were all I happened to have on at that moment. What a vision.

The truth was, I had long since outgrown anything resem-bling what you would normally call panties. What I could fit in at this point looked more like pillowcases. I had to hide them from MoonPie; whenever he would find a pair of them, he would throw them away. I knew what he was thinking: If he could just get rid of all the big ones, I'd be forced to buy new—and small and sexy—undies. Typically male in his think-ing, he never looked at the big picture—that's how we ended up pregnant to start with. I bet if you researched it, you'd find out that all the pretty underwear factories are owned by gangs of obstetricians. Everything's a plot, I swear.

But anyway, I wasn't wearing any panties of any kind in order to avoid that pesky visible panty line. Now, why on earth I thought anybody would be looking at my butt—well, preg-nant women are not always rational. Anyway, Pie walked in and was surprised that I wasn't wearing anything under my tights: "You're not wearing any panties?" I didn't hesitate, nor did I even look up at him. I just said, real offhand, "Oh, you never wear panties to a party," and kept on doing whatever. He just stood there, slack-jawed, for a full thirty seconds, considering the implications, I suppose. I had moved on, forgotten about it, and he was still standing there, gaping. "You don't? Nobody does?" "Nobody does what?" I asked him. "Panties to a party—doesn't anybody wear 'em?" He was looking sort of dreamy and clearly thought he was being let in on some big secret of all womankind: that every party he'd ever been to or would ever go to—there wasn't a pair of panties in the room—and he was the only guy who knew.

He was so highly entertained at the prospect, the Queens tried it on some other husbands and fiancés with comparable results. So we made it a rule: Never wear panties to a party. But there's no point in not wearing panties if nobody knows you're not wearing panties, so be sure to tell someone. You will know instinctively with whom to share this information.

Sometimes you just don't know how much preparedness will be required. A girlfriend of mine went to the Y to work out. Feeling rather sporty in her workout gear, she sauntered out to the front desk area to chat with new arrivals. After a surfeit of small talk and gooning guys, she was ready to hit the track.

Be Prepared

Since it was still a bit chilly outside, she put on her sweatshirt. Somehow, in one of those flukes that you could never recreate in a million years, a pair of pantyhose that had been lurking in the depths of the sweatshirt somehow contrived to thrust themselves up and out the neckhole and fly fifteen or so feet across the crowded lobby, landing smack on the counter in front of some unsuspecting guy just standing there waiting for some towels. Great little ice-breaker, I thought. (I must remember it—odd we hadn't thought of it before.) For years women have been hurling their underwear at rock stars on stages all over the world. Why not bring this time-honored tradition down to a more day-to-day application, where it might actually accomplish an introduction, at the very least?

Actually, come to think of it, I did already think of it. Many moons ago, long before the advent of postpartum underwear, when MoonPie was still ardently earning his name and thought that the sun shone from various orifices of my person, we happened to be in the Paradise Café in Grayton Beach, Florida. MoonPie got his name because you know when you fall in love and feel so great and act so goofy and mushy—that's being moonpied. (A Moon Pie is a gigantic, gooshy, chocolate-covered-marshmallow-graham-cracker deal that we are inordinately fond of in the South. Moon Pies are often consumed in conjunction with either a cola-type drink or an orange-flavored soda—as in a "Moon Pie an' a Ah-ra-Cee-co-cola" or a "Moon Pie an' a Big Ahrnge.")

So anyway, he was moonpied bigtime, and I, of course, found this gratifying. So at some point, after the salad and before the entrée, I excused myself to the powder room. When I returned, I leaned across the table and pressed something into MoonPie's hand. It was, of course, my panties—which, at that particular juncture in my life, were very small, pink, and lacy—completely unlike the aforementioned "married" variety. Needless to say, it was a very short meal. I recall go-boxes being ordered forthwith. So as I ponder this memory, I can assure you that lingerie-flinging can have felicitous results, and I recommend it to you highly. There is a lot to be said for timing and technique in this business of preparedness.

A good case could also be made for carrying around with you your toothbrush, a change of underwear, a large supply of your chosen method of protection, your favorite pillow, and perhaps even a small canned ham. Our good friend Larry Bouchea showed up at a Queens' gathering recently and pulled out of his pocket the tiniest little canned ham we ever saw. "Oh!" we cried in delight, "it's a *pocket ham*!" We were so taken with the idea that we've included it in our Be Prepared Kit. You can, and we hope you will, visit our website at www.sweetpotatoqueens.com and order your own Be Prepared Kit. Some may feel that a pocket ham moves one beyond simply being Optimistically Prepared and into the realm of Predatory Anticipation. We feel that this is a matter of personal conscience and we would come down hard on the

pro-choice side. After a pretty bad streak of men, we even considered amending the list to include carrying some sort of
weapon, also because you just never know. If there exists in
this universe anything more infuriating and crazy-making than
a man, I don't know what it is, thank you, and I don't want to
know. Of course, on a good day, I would also have to say if
there is anything in this universe *better* than a man, I don't
know what it is; and I don't think it would even be healthful
for me to know at this stage of my life.

But if you've decided to go out on a limb and kill one, for
goodness' sake, be prepared. We all read, with dismay, the sad
story of a good woman wronged in south Mississippi who took
that option and made a complete mess of the entire thing. See,
first she shot him. Well, she saw right off the bat that that was
a mistake because then she had this enormous dead body to
deal with. He was every bit as much trouble to her dead as he
ever had been alive, and he was getting more so all the time.
So then she made another snap decision to cut him up in
pieces and dispose of him a hunk at a time. More poor planning. First she didn't have the proper carving utensils on hand,
and hacking him up proved to be just a major chore, plus it
made just this colossal mess on her off-white shag living room
carpet. It's getting to be like the Cat in the Hat now, only
Thing Two ain't showing up to help with the cleanup. She
finally gets him into portable-size portions, and wouldn't you
know it? Cheap trash bags. Can anything else possible go

wrong for this poor woman? So the lesson here is obvious—for want of a small chain saw, a roll of Visqueen, and some genuine Hefty bags, she is in Parchman Penitentiary today instead of New Orleans, where she'd planned to go with her new boyfriend. Preparation is everything. However, if you have been particular, you shouldn't need to be prepared to this extreme. Try to avoid getting involved with somebody who's gonna need killing before it's over. It may seem to you that that narrows the field somewhat, but be diligent.

So moved were the Sweet Potato Queens by this woman's plight that we swore a mighty oath that it would never happen to us, no, not to us nor to any of our people. Since that time, whenever one of us gets married, which seems to be a pretty regular occurrence for some unfathomable reason, we make sure that all the basics of preparedness are covered at the bridal shower. Chain saws and garbage bags are only the beginning. The centerpiece is traditional: an extremely large (I'd say about three feet tall, and a foot or so in diameter) inflatable penis. This lends a festive air to the occasion. Many Fat Mama's Knock You Naked Margaritas are prepared and cheerfully consumed. The bride is presented with the catalog from our favorite store, The Pleasure Chest, whose Los Angeles location we frequent whenever possible. The Queens are quite Clampett-like in their wide-eyed wonder at the incredible array of exotic devices on display. We had never even heard of a butt-plug, and here we were, faced with an entire butt-plug department in a retail establishment. We were quite carried away with the assortment of tit clamps available as well. Tammy's favorite was actually the cheapest model available—seven dollars—an old-fashioned wooden clothespin—painted black!

The bride (and whoever else needs one) also gets the Good Vibrations catalog. This is actually a very educational book, and the Queens feel *very* strongly about education. We learned, thanks to our dear friends at Good Vibrations, that the vibrator was invented in the late nineteenth century—in America, of course—by doctors for treating "female disorders." It seems that genital massage was SMP (standard medical practice) at that time, to induce what they called "hysterical paroxysm." We like to call it "orgasm" today. The vibrator was invented to be a labor-saving device for the doctors! And quite the little time-saver, too, I expect. You got twenty women in the waiting room who want to get off before you can play golf—you got to come up with a better way. We were not in the least surprised to hear that men were in too big a hurry to fool with us, even in that slower era. That one of the greatest boons to womankind was actually invented to make life easier for men is okay by us.

According to the Good Vibes folks, it didn't take long for this handy-dandy new apparatus to show up for sale in women's mags and mail-order catalogs. It was touted as a cureall for headaches, asthma, "fading beauty," and tuberculosis. We would like to offer our personal testimony as to the efficacy of these happy little machines: Our headaches are gone, our asthma cleared up, our beauty actually *needs* to fade a bit to make it safer for us to go out in public, and not one of the Queens has ever had TB. We must say, those vibrator manufacturers are some creative little buggers.

We pass the catalogs around, and everybody gets a chance to pick out the models she finds most intriguing. There is a lot of reading aloud. There are a few consistent crowd pleasers: the Auto-arouser, which plugs into your car's cigarette lighter and promises to add a whole new dimension to road trips, and the Butterfly, which is apparently a little deal that you can actually wear under your clothes, say, to work, to keep you vibrant during those wretchedly boring staff meetings. We think these butterfly devices should be standard issue for all postal workers—indeed, all government employees, and anybody else who has to deal with the public. On reflection, wouldn't the world be a better place if we all wore one? In fact, if we all wore them long enough, could we not expect some natural form of butterfly vibrator to evolve into our species? And isn't it strange that with all the attention He/She devoted to detail (strawberries, for example—who but God could have come up with those?), we are not already so equipped? The only possible explanation we can come up with for this glaring lapse is that not even God could have predicted at Creation just how far over time we humans would stray from the path.

But anyway, we provide the bride with the means for obtaining whatever marital aids she personally feels will aid her the most, and we do not force her to share with the group what exactly those might be. We restrict our gifts to things we know for certain she will need: the smallest, most beautiful lingerie ever created, and high-heeled satin slippers with marabou trim.

There will be those days, however, when none of these items of preparedness are sufficient. Not pretty panties or married panties or no panties. Shaved legs won't matter, and even butterfly vibrators will do you no good. And even if you have a chain saw, you won't be able to get to it. Sometimes the only thing that will work is your own ingenuity. And this brings us to the last and most important rule: *Be creative.*

Before Xena, There Was Curtisene

The very essence of creative preparedness is contained in the person of Curtisene Lloyd, and for this reason she is the unchallenged winner of the Sweet Potato Queens' highest award: *The Most Prepared Woman the World Has Ever Known.* (Every word of the story I am about to tell you is true. It is authenticated in court documents.) Curtisene Lloyd is a mild-mannered, sweet-voiced little Sunday school teacher of a lady, middle-aged, a nurse. She lives, with her very old deaf aunt, in a nice house in a little town not far from Jackson, where she works at a large hospital.

February 1990. Late one night Curtisene awoke to discover a man in her bedroom. And he was definitely not there at her invitation. This intruder advised her of the various and sundry obscene things he planned to do to her before he made up his mind whether or not he would kill her. "I might kill you," he said, "but I'm gone git me summa dis fust." And with that he removed all of his clothing and climbed up on the bed. He situated himself on the headboard somehow and began giving Curtisene some rather detailed instructions concerning the performance he expected from her.

Now, our Curtisene, she was paying real close attention. She had taken note right off that this guy did not have any sort of weapon with him. And then she did something that never in his worst nightmares had he dreamed she would do. She just reached out and took *aholt*. She did. Our Curtisene grabbed a hold, and then she commenced to twisting. She got both hands on his merchandise, and she twisted—in opposite directions at the same time with as much force as she could muster.

Apparently it was sufficient. Her attacker beat her about the head and shoulders and struggled frantically to get free of this death grip, but Curtisene was on him like all those time-honored phrases you've heard all your life—white on rice, duck on a June bug, and so on.

So, still holding fast, she drags him, now sniveling and crying, through the house, where her little old deaf aunt is sleeping in peaceful oblivion. He's begging her to let go:

"Let go and call the po-leece! Just let go!" He's swearing he's dying.

"No, you ain't dying," she says back to him. "I'm trying to kill you, but you won't die."

He promises he'll leave if only she will, please God, let him go.

"Fine," she says, "go on then. Leave."

He's crying and saying he *cain't* and how can he when she won't let him go?

To which our Curtisene casually replies, "You broke in, didn't you, sumbitch? Break out!"

He is wailing to beat the band, and she is dragging him to the front door. She tells him there are three locks on that door that he'll have to open in order to make good his escape. He is pretty much a lifeless heap by now, except for the bawling. She hoists him up to open the first lock. He gets it open and falls back to the floor. "He was starting to wheeze a little by this time," Curtisene reported.

He's crying and saying how much she's got him suffering, to which she snappily replies, "How 'bout all that suffering you were fixing to put on me?" She tells him he's got two more locks, if you please. She hoists him up, and he thinks he's out.

"Nope. The screen's latched," Curtisene tells him.

And up he goes again. And he's sure he's free now. At this point, she later confessed to the jury—in the shyest little voice you ever heard, like she was letting you in on a little secret— "I kinda worked on him a little bit." Meaning, if it had been possible to twist his genitalia completely off his body, she would have accomplished that feat at the end of her front porch.

And then she repeated to those assembled her final words to the man: "I'm takin' you to the end of the porch, and then I'm gon' go back in the house and get my gun, and I'm gon' blow your m——f——g head off, you slimy, stanking, low-down piece of shit, you!" As she repeated those words, clear as a bell, in open court, you could feel, in every living soul in that courtroom, an almost overwhelming desire to stand up and cheer.

What happened to the rapist wannabe? Well, he limped off through the bushes, but he wasn't hard for the police to find. Especially since he departed buck nekkid and left all his clothes in her bedroom—with his full name written on the labels inside. He was also pretty easy to spot in the lineup: He was the one who didn't stand up straight. He may never stand up straight again, actually. And don't you just know he was a big man in jail, after the truth came out. Little-bitty Sunday school teacher just waxed his ass.

Curtisene Lloyd did not get the standing ovation that her testimony so richly deserved—courtroom decorum and all that—but every single person in the courtroom that day went up to her afterward and said, "Miss Lloyd, I just want to shake your hand."

Curtisene Lloyd, my hero. I love this woman, the Most Prepared Woman the World Has Ever Known.

5

Educating Our Young

IN A MANNER MOST BEFITTING A QUEEN

I have a preteen daughter who was nicknamed BoPeep by the Queens' Official Consort, Lance Romance, while she was still incubating inside my spacious midsection. His theory was that as a child of the Sweet Potato Queens, she should not have a name overused by the masses. As far as we know, there's been only one other female with this particular name in the history of the world. My daughter doesn't have to worry about which Sarah or Amanda or Melissa they're calling because she ain't one of 'em. Bringing up 'Peep in a manner befitting the daughter of a Queen has been no small task.

Understanding pageants is an essential part of the curriculum. The Queens have a love-hate relationship with pageants. First the hate part. We hate the thought of females of any age—but certainly the younger they are, the worse it is (their mamas should be clubbed to death with cans of Aqua-Net)—posturing, preening, groveling, if you will, for meaningless titles with no accompanying power and appallingly cheap crowns from crass promoters with dubious agendas. It's too embarrassing for words. But we do love to watch them do it. I mean, we really love pageants.

Whenever there's a pageant of any kind on TV, we all gather at my house for the Pageant Party. This means the standard many margaritas and large quantities of food. I have a personal arsenal of rubber dart guns, and everybody selects the weapon of her choice and gets a pile of darts. Then bring on them beauties! Our favorite part is the opening cattle call, especially when the contestants wear some sort of costume representative of their home base. In one state pageant we got to see two grown women dressed, respectively, as a recliner and a small aircraft. In the year that will forever dwell in our hearts, we got a hula dancer, a marimba player, a clogger, and one girl who danced barefoot on broken glass to "The Battle Hymn of the Republic" as performed by Elvis Presley. Pageants with talent competitions are obviously preferred.

Educating Our Young

The darts fly as the spirit moves us. Sometimes the TV will be one solid mass of darts, and sometimes only a solitary missile will be launched, but we have a wholesome good time at the expense of the trick-dog contestants locked in mortal combat for those scholarships. I'm personally grateful they'll do anything for a crown.

Growing up in a house where Pageant Parties are a regular occurrence was confusing to young 'Peep in the beginning. She would sit, observe all this frenzy from the sidelines, and ask, in her sweet little-girl voice, "Why are y'all making fun of 'em, Mama? They're so pretty, and I like those sparkly dresses, Mama." We took this as our opportunity to begin educating her properly, hoping to nip the bud of this pageant thing, at least in our own home. We explained to her that yes, they're pretty. We're all pretty, thankfully. It is a good thing to be pretty. But we are not *just* pretty, and pretty all by itself is not worth much since it lasts only about an hour, relative to the rest of your life. In addition, pretty is just a major accident of birth, and nobody can take any personal credit for it (except when it's bought and paid for at the plastic guy's office, but never mind that). They shouldn't be handing out awards for being lucky enough to not be born a dogball, I tell her.

Life holds few pleasures, if any, more exalted than riding on a float in a sparkly dress with a crown on one's head, I admit to her. What matters, however, is *how* you *get* that crown. We're not about to do tricks on national TV for a crown. In life, I tell her, it's vitally important that you buy your own crown and declare yourself Queen, and then spend the rest of your life living into that. Pretty will last a short time, at best, but stupid can last forever. Fortunately, so can smart.

Are You Quite Certain You Have the Upper Hand?

The Sweet Potato Queens Educational Program extends far beyond beauty pageants and crowns, however. As with all good mothers, discipline is important to us. We are against hitting children. My father always said this really annoying but true thing to my mother, and it always pissed her off because it was so true: "If you can't control yourself, you can't control a child." We think it takes craft and wiles to raise children effectively without creating a mutant race of sheep-kids who will meekly comply with any command from any adult. Spare us those mealymouthed little "yes ma'am, no sir" robots. We know that they've been literally beaten into submission. We also know that they are inwardly seething, and there will be hell to pay one fine day.

What I always did with BoPeep on the extremely rare occasions when she was acting buttheaded in public: I'd squat down right beside her and get right in her little ear and say, real low and contained, often through clenched teeth (I've found that just about anything you say through clenched teeth takes on an added tone of pith and import), "You are acting awful, and it's embarrassing me, and if you don't stop on a dime, then in about two seconds *I* am going to do something that will embarrass *you* so much, I doubt seriously you'll ever completely recover." Presto! She would immediately revert to being the perfect child. I never had to *do* anything and actually never had any idea of what exactly I would do, if she called my bluff. It's never happened. I figure that, having grown up watching me doing any number of things she considered humiliating when I was in a good mood, she was so terrified when I was in an angry one that the prospect was unthinkable to her.

But witness what can happen to you when discipline goes awry. This is, sadly, a true story. An unidentified mom is attempting to conduct a banking transaction in a downtown bank, during lunch hour, on a Friday. Only a few thousand people are in there. Her kid is running all over, being your basic four-year-old asshole. Mom loses her place in line about fifty times chasing the little beester down. Finally she's almost up to the teller's window, when she looks around and sees Beester on the far side of the bank on top of a loan officer's desk, rummaging, pillaging, and stomping around. So she shrieks across the bank, "*Beester!* If you don't get down from there and get over here *right now*, I am gonna *blister your bottom!*" To which Beester retorts, at the top of his little lungs from his highly visible vantage point atop the officer's desk, "No, you won't neither! 'Cause if you do, I'm gonna tell Meemaw that I saw you put your mouth on Daddy's weenie!"

Talk about your slam-dunk. I have no idea what the fate of the hapless Beester was, but Mom dissolved on the spot into a little greasy puddle and evaporated into the air. What else could she do under the circumstances? But doesn't this kid have leverage forever? I'm talking bulletproof for life.

Regarding Prejudice and Religion

When my sister, Judy, was in the first grade, they had those double desks, and her desk mate was, of all things, a boy. This in itself was hardly to be tolerated, but to make matters worse, he smelled "funny." In the forty-some-odd years I've known my sister, I've never been able to ascertain what "funny" meant, and so I have no idea what he smelled like. Well, it seems that he also had red hair, and since he was the only red-headed person she had ever encountered and he smelled funny, little first-grade Judy extrapolated that redheaded people smell funny—all of them. And she is now, well, she's a lot older than she used to be, and she still believes that. It's a basic corollary of life for her. Until the day she dies, she will maintain that redheaded people smell funny, and she can't be persuaded otherwise.

I, too, had a vivid prejudice-forming experience as a small

child. There was a family on the street where I grew up who belonged to some off-brand of church that called itself Baptist. These folks were four-plus crazy, in my opinion. They had all these bizarre rules for all aspects of life, such as: Nobody may wear shorts on Sunday. Now, I couldn't have been over six or seven years old, but I distinctly remember thinking that that was the stupidest rule I had ever heard. With all the terrible things going on in the world—the only ones I can remember being well informed on were the starving children in China and World Communism, but I was properly horrified by both of those—all God's got to worry about is whether or not Lindy and Mindy are wearing shorts on Sunday? I thought if that turned out to be true, my opinion of God was gonna drop a notch or two. So I asked the fount of all wisdom, Daddy, what he thought about it. He pursed up his lips and twinkled a bit around the eyes and replied: "Some people must think God's stupid."

So growing up, I just knew I might become a lot of things, but I knew I never wanted to be a Baptist. Then I grew up and could fully understand that all Baptists didn't believe such nutty things; but a trace of my old prejudice lingers still, and I'm always on guard in the presence of known Baptists.

The point of all this is to demonstrate how easily lifelong prejudices can be formed by the silliest of circumstances. Therefore we feel it is important that our children be taught this simple tenet: Hate people on an individual basis only—

you must actually get to know someone at least slightly before you can properly hate him or her.

My daddy told about an old man who lived in Kosciusko when Daddy was a little boy. This man was locally famous for his favorite oath. Whenever he told a tale that was particularly unbelievable to his listeners, he would end it by saying, "And if that ain't so, then God's a possum!" Devout members of his audience would gasp and step back to avoid the lightning they felt sure was about to strike the man. It never did, of course, and this demonstrated definitive proof to me and my daddy that God has a great sense of humor. We Queens always feel lucky in that regard since we make fun of everything.

In the Jackson neighborhood where I grew up, not only was the Baptist count high, there were also some off-brand cult types—all ultrareligious. When tempers would erupt during a game of chase or hide-and-go-seek, the children of these off-brands would splutter and stammer in anger, too young and inexperienced to know how to cuss each other out properly. When matters finally really reached the boiling point, right before blows were to be exchanged, one would yell at the other, *"You don't know your Ten Commandments!"* It always came out sounding like one word, *"Tinkamandments."* And the battle would be on. I'd watch all this and muse, "Now, I wonder what God thinks about this?"

Educating Our Young

In trying to provide some spiritual guidance for your kid, I swear, weeding out undesirable elements—or garbage, as I like to call it—takes almost as much energy as dispensing the good stuff. There have been a number of religious groups in recent years that I've found wildly entertaining. One of my preferences was that woman who claimed her body would be sporadically taken over by the spirit of a 35,000-year-old warrior. She made about a gabillion dollars with this. I'm sick I didn't think of it. I saw a video of her. Considering myself to be pretty open-minded about spiritual matters, I sat down to watch, casting aside any judgment about the probability of a 35,000-year-old warrior randomly inhabiting the person of a middle-aged woman from Montana.

The woman on the video came out quietly, almost demurely, in flowing white pajamas, and stood before a big wicker papasan chair. The audience (a couple of hundred believers who had paid about $750 each) sat in rapt silence. She addressed them briefly, in the softest little voice you ever heard. Then she sat down in the chair, took a couple of deep breaths, and slumped forward in a "trance." All of this took no more than eight seconds, I swear. Then, in the "trance," she sprang up out of the chair and began striding forcefully about the stage, pausing every now and then to strike a pose that looked not a little like Yul Brynner in *The King and I*. As a matter of fact, everything she said and did, right down to the pajamas, was a straight rip-off of Yul Brynner in *The King and I*. Her pronouncements, delivered in Yul Brynner's voice, were on a level of profundity with "The book is brown" or "Potatoes are good." I don't know whatever became of that woman, but my guess is she is somewhere, rich as all get out and pretty happy about it.

Then we had those Heaven's Gate people. I never did really understand their deal completely, but it had something to do with them all killing themselves and hitching a ride to Heaven on the Hale-Bopp comet when it swung by. Who came up with this theory? Whoever it was put in some interesting details for the group to follow. Apparently they were to kill themselves because they wouldn't be needing their "containers," or bodies, as we laypersons call them. Despite the fact that the "containers" would not be needed, it was imperative that all "containers" look exactly alike—same clothes, same goofy haircut, and so on. When all the identical "containers" were discovered dead as nails, each of them had a big sack of quarters nearby. Let me understand this. In Heaven we don't need our bodies, but we do need quarters? If Heaven turns out to be a place governed by a bunch of folks who demand that not only must all people look alike and dress alike but also have exact change, forget about it—I'm hereby canceling my reservation. Sounds suspiciously like Hell to me.

Regarding people who endlessly pass judgment on others

and proclaim loudly, as if they know, who will and who won't be in Heaven and why, my daddy always said, "Last time I checked, your name wasn't listed on the 'range-mints [arrangements] committee." Meaning thank God, you're not the boss of anything. One of our very dearest Baptist buddies told us one morning that she'd never go to a nude beach on account of the rapture might come, and there she'd be with a bunch of naked people! I said, Well, if it comes anytime soon, I hope I'm sleeping; everybody looks innocent when asleep. If God wasn't mightily amused by our humanness, I figure he'd have wiped us out a long time ago.

Making Mama Proud

"How yew gon' ack win yew git sumware?" is a question often asked—or "axed," depending on your neighborhood—of all Southern children—or "chirren." Knowing and then cheerfully doing the right thing in all social situations is a burden that weighs heavily on the children of Southern mothers. Any failure on our part to know and do the right thing is no reflection on us, personally, even if we happen to be fifty-five years old and our mamas have been dead for thirty years at least. No, if we commit some unspeakable social faux pas (often pronounced *foo paw* here), the blame for it will be placed at the door of our mamas. It's not bad enough that we actually threw up in the azalea bushes in the front yard of the Governor's

Mansion; the truly bad thing is that someone saw us and told not only our mamas but our mamas' friends. And it's no help to tell Mama that the only reason that rat saw us throwing up in the azalea bushes in front of the Governor's Mansion was because he nearly ran over us making his exit via the governor's flower garden in an erratically driven automobile. He's the one who got arrested. Does that help our cause one speck? It does not. Let *his* mama suffer that particular shame; we're discussing our own. And now, thanks to us, our mama cannot look anyone in the eye, so shamed is she by our behavior.

Being a source of embarrassment to your mama is just about the worst thing that can happen to you around here, unless, of course, whatever you did happens to make a whole lot of money. The wish for fortune is the only reason I'm able to sit down and actually write this book. I can assure you that my mama and all her friends will be properly horrified at its contents, except for the parts that they won't understand. I told the other Queens when I started this book, "Well, girls, it looks like it's time we explain to our mamas that we've been promising people blow jobs for the last twelve years." Most of us then had to explain what a blow job was and, furthermore, why men find them so desirable. As predicted, all the mothers were indeed horrified. However, they are somewhat mollified by the prospect of profit. It's okay to humiliate the family if it pays well—sort of an extension of the beauty pageant notion "anything for a crown." If I fail to make sufficient money from the sale of this epistle, however, I'll not only become the poster woman for immoral scum who have embarrassed their mamas. I'll no doubt be targeted for special visitation by the Jehovah's Witnesses. (A good pal of mine loves for the Witnesses to come to his door. He graciously ushers them inside, prepares refreshments, and bids them to tell their story. But first he'll say, "Write down your name and address for me because tomorrow I'm gonna drop by your house and tell you what all *I* think about religion." They can't get out of there fast enough.)

Two Tough Tests for Etiquette

My dear departed friend Beth Jones, a college English professor, related to me a story that is fraught with etiquette dilemmas. Beth swore to me that the star of this show was not Beth herself but a friend. I've always had my doubts, but as Beth is not here to defend herself, we'll grant that this happened to someone else. Beth's friend had to travel to another city on business. As it happened, Beth had other friends living in that particular city, so she arranged for her friend to stay in the home of these other friends. Beth's Jackson friend arrived at the other friends' house in time for dinner, and a jovial time was had by all.

By and by, after dinner Beth's friend was shown to her

quarters for the night, the guest room. During the night the guest was awakened by a call of nature. Now, if memory served her correctly, the facilities adjoined her hosts' bedroom, which in turn adjoined *her* room. This meant that she'd have to go through their bedroom in the middle of the night to reach the potty. She was in a fair quandary, Beth's friend was. She didn't want to walk into these people's bedroom unannounced in the wee, wee hours. Nor did she want to knock on the door. She didn't want to wake them if they were sleeping, much less walk in on any late-night activities. What was she to do? By this time, she was practically dancing a jig, she had to pee so bad. Out of utter desperation, an idea came to her, and she went into the other room that adjoined hers, the kitchen. She felt around in the dark for a very large bowl she had earlier noticed sitting on the counter and found it. And yes, she did just what you're afraid I'm going to tell you she did. And with great relief, I might add. But alas, her relief was to be short-lived. For just as she was comfortably midstream, all the lights blazed on, and there stood her hosts, staring in bewildered disbelief at this grown woman squatting over and urinating into their very large mixing bowl.

Suffice it to say that nobody concerned knew quite how to respond to the situation they found themselves in. What can you, the hosts, say to a houseguest whom you met only a few hours ago and have just discovered whizzing in your dishes? What would Emily Post say? Miss Manners? What can you, the houseguest, say to your hosts, to whom you were introduced only hours ago, who have found you whizzing in their dishes? Her heart had been in the right place: She truly did not want to disturb them, no matter what they were doing. We think, however, they were perhaps a tad more upset by what resulted. Given the choice of having her knock on their door, barge right in, or weewee in the Wedgwood, I'd bet my money they'd pick hands down one of the first two options.

There are just some situations—I don't care how vigilant your mama was about teaching you manners—that will throw everybody's learning for a loop.

One time one of the Queens, Tammy, and I were out for our early-morning walk around the track at the Y where we work out. Tammy was in a major funk about something, and I'd been practically tap-dancing around the track, trying in vain to perk her up. I was pulling out all my best stuff, and nothing was working. And then I glanced off to the right, behind Tammy, into the parking lot of the hotel at the other end of the track. Under the brilliant beam of the streetlight stood...a *nekkid* man. Now, I say nekkid because that's what he was. There's a profound difference between naked and nekkid. Naked is proud, noble, graceful, without shame or the need for it. Nekkid is, on the other hand...well, it's nekkid.

And so I said to Tammy, "There's a nekkid man." We paused momentarily while she turned to look.

She nodded in agreement. "There certainly is."

He was just strolling along, not a care in the world, not a stitch on. He made no effort whatsoever to conceal his parts, although I saw nothing worthy of so ostentatious a public display. About this time he looked our way. Tammy said cheerily, "Hi!"

"Hi!" he said. "How are y'all this mornin'?"

"Oh, much better now, thank you," she replied, the absolute soul of politeness. The nekkid man seemed to appreciate her gracious attitude.

You see, in this very small verbal exchange, Tammy upheld not only the sacred doctrine of Southern hospitality but the very highest standard of the Sweet Potato Queens. She spoke kindly to the man, regardless of his race, creed, color, religion, social status, or appearance, which was nekkid. I was proud to call her my friend. I hope BoPeep turns out so well.

6

He Ain't Nothin' But a Man

YOU BETTER HAVE A GOOD DEFENSE

Once upon a time I was passing through Carthage, Mississippi, on my way to the Neshoba County Fair, which is held near Philadelphia, Mississippi. The Neshoba County Fair is called the "Giant Houseparty." That is somewhat misleading, but the truth would take too many words, and it doesn't really matter because no new people can come to it anyway. Here's the deal with the Neshoba County Fair: A hundred-some-odd years ago, for reasons long lost in the mists of time, a bunch of people went to the county fairgrounds in Neshoba County and built themselves a whole passel of shacks that they would then go live in for one week once a year when the fair came. That particular week always happened to fall around the last week of July, first week of August, depending. Depending on what, I have never figured out. Loosely translated for people in more temperate climes: Fair Week is hotter than the hammered-down hinges of Hell. Somehow it caught on, though, this week of shack-dwelling, and it has continued unto this very day and time. It has become a part of my life, and I can't even remember how or why.

Once a year, for a couple of weeks in July, I am driven by unseen forces to cook like a fiend the most fattening casseroles I can think of, freeze them all, and cook more. Then I'm forced to load all the food and BoPeep into the car and head for the red dirt hills of Neshoba County to live in a two-story, unair-conditioned shack with about thirty people and one bathroom. Once there I unload all the food and discuss with Lallah Perry, the owner of our particular shack, what dishes should be thawed for dinner that night. Eating is the primary fair entertainment for those who don't favor alcohol poisoning.

Whether you are an eater or a drinker, the drill is the same: You do all you can stand to do at one sitting in your own cabin. Then you go sit on the porch until you can recover enough to walk. After that you go to another cabin and repeat the drill. Sooner or later you usually wind up back at your original cabin, where you go upstairs to your assigned bed and rest up for the next day's activities, which are identical to the ones you just completed. Sometimes it happens that folks don't make it back to their home cabin and assigned bed. Sometimes they end up wedged behind a door for the night or underneath a stranger on the infield of the racetrack or the ninth hole of the golf course, which is not even close to the fairgrounds. But these would be exceptions to the rule, and hey, it's Fair Week, so it doesn't really count. Everybody is *so* laid back and friendly, you'd really have to go out of your way to piss somebody off.

Two years ago I wandered up in one cabin, not knowing a soul, and struck up a conversation with the lady of the shack and somehow worked into the conversation that I wished I had a whole bunch of deviled eggs, and did she happen to have any? She said she didn't have any but she'd be happy to whip up a couple dozen if I didn't mind going to borrow some mustard since she was out of it. So I said I wouldn't mind a bit, and while she set about boiling a big ole pot of eggs, I headed out to go door-to-door of other cabins in which I didn't know a soul, asking could I please borrow their mustard so Sylvia Mars could make me some deviled eggs. I'll have you know that the folks in the first cabin that happened to have some plain old yellow mustard were just thrilled to loan it to me, and they never even asked if they could have some of the deviled eggs, too. I trotted back with the mustard, and Sylvia made me those eggs. I ate a fair bait of 'em and bid her a fond farewell and didn't see her again until the fair the next year.

When I stopped by her cabin to say "Hidee!" she sort of looked blank, and I reminded her that she didn't really know me but she had made me a batch of deviled eggs last year, and she said, "Oh, of course, come on in, how are you?" And we sat and visited like old chums. I certainly do consider Sylvia Mars to be one of my best friends on account of those eggs. Do you have any idea how much trouble it is to make deviled eggs? A lot, which is why I hadn't already made them myself. Well, that's just the kind of stuff that goes on at the fair. And that's why people have been going for a hundred-some-odd years.

And as I was passing through Carthage on my way to the fair one year, I stopped for a Little Something at the Crestview Dairy Bar. That is the ice cream store that looks for all the world like a bank. I went in and placed my order for a Little Something. I happened to be wearing one of my favorite T-shirts. I have one that says, "You Are Dumb." I love that one. I have one that says, "Men Are All Idiots and I Am Married to Their King." That's a real favorite, too. But the one I had on that day read, "My Next Husband Will Be Normal." Well, the little old lady behind the counter just about fell over laughing at my T-shirt. She was walking up and down back there, laughing and talking to herself. "I don't know what in the world all these girls are thinkin' of these days, gettin' married; they must just like changin' their names—you cain't make nothin' but a *man* out of 'em. And I don't care *who* he is when you git 'im home, they's somethin' *bad* wrong with 'im!"

Really, we Queens love men. They taste just like chicken. Well, we can't really say that for a fact. The ones we've actually bitten were not only not cooked properly, they were alive and kicking. Shrieking, as it were. In our defense I would have to say that they deserved it, and in retrospect I imagine even they would agree. But anyway, we do love men. In theory at least. I mean, they do sound great on paper, don't they? And we are quite the eternal optimists, we are. Even when there are no serious contenders in the game, we like to have a number of men on hand. Just to play with, you know. We think of them as cat toys.

We've had a lot of experience with men who were looking for Barbie and the Dreamhouse. All men want Barbie. It's certainly easy enough to see why—I mean, her feet won't even go flat. She wears spike heels, more commonly known as FMPs, all the time. (That's F——— Me Pumps, for the undereducated.) Even if she has on tennis shoes, Barbie's feet are standing on tiptoes inside the tennis shoes. Show me the man who claims to be unmoved by the sight of a woman in high-heeled shoes, and I'll show you a liar—and a fool, too, if he thinks anybody believes him.

Look at Barbie's body. No, really *look* at it. Notice that impossibly fabulous shape. Then become aware that it is only a shape—she has no actual body parts that could possibly require outside attention. She is like a 3-D centerfold. She cannot see, hear, feel, or, best of all, speak. Another big plus is that permanent pleasant expression on her face. (Alas, even Barbie has a drawback. You'll notice that Barbie, perfect as she is, could not perform a blow job on a bet.)

And so here is the universal male fantasy: He is sitting— make that *lying*—on the couch, watching [insert appropriate sport] on the biggest big screen TV ever made. You are in the kitchen, wearing an outfit that amounts to Band-Aids and high heels, while cooking obscene amounts of extremely fattening food for him. You serve this food, along with buckets of beer, in the TV room. You bend over a lot in your little outfit. When all the food and all the beer is gone, you give him a blow job. He falls asleep, and while he is sleeping, you clean up the house and iron all his clothes, including his underwear, and then you leave. You have performed all of this without ever uttering a word. You appear, unbidden, as if by sorcery, on a regular basis to perform this little ritual. His level of partici- pation is strictly that of happy, passive recipient. This is what is known as Barbie's Dreamhouse.

Men get all pissed off if you accuse them of wanting Bar- bie. This is only because they can tell from your tone of voice that you perceive this to be a negative character trait in them.

They haven't the foggiest idea why this would be a negative character trait—I mean, we're talking Barbie here, what's not to like? Right? But you are frowning when you say it and looking at him like he just crawled out from under a rock, so he instinctively knows that this is a bad thing, and his knee-jerk reaction is to deny, deny, deny.

Not that any of us would disparage a defense based solely on denial. We are all in favor of it and have used it satisfactorily on many occasions ourselves. In fact, Tammy, our own personal Queen of Mean, has taken it one step further. She has taken your basic denial defense, which pretty much states that, even if you are caught in the act of whatever, red-handed, as it were—just look 'em in the eye and de-ny, de-ny, de-ny: "Who are you gonna believe—me, or your lying eyes?" Tammy's twist on that is she doesn't stay too long in the denial mode. No, our Tammy makes her denial statement with a look that says, "No, not me. I would never," moving almost simultaneously into "Why would I?" and then, looking just as wide-eyed as you please, into "How could you even think such a thing?"

At this point something just comes over her. That sweet look of wounded innocence is gone so fast, it makes you woozy. In its place is the Tasmanian Devil. She gets all fuzzed-up and wild-looking, you can feel it coming from her toes, you can see it behind her eyes, and then she just explodes. "You m——f——r!" she screams at him. This catches him off guard, as you may well imagine since, if you'll recall, *she* is the one who just got caught. He had been seeing himself as the injured party in all this. What is she yelling at him for? In that split second—when he's distracted and his thoughts are racing, trying to figure out if, in fact, he has done something and forgotten about it and now she's discovered it and what the hell could it be?—in that nanosecond the wind changes. The tide turns. Advantage Tammy.

She just lets fly. None of this makes any sense—doesn't have to. It's just like yelling at your dog. He has no earthly idea what you're talking about, but he does understand that he is in big trouble. This is known as the "you m——f——r" defense, and it should be used only in dire emergencies. It is not for the faint of heart. To achieve maximum effectiveness with this approach, you have to be prepared to pull out all the stops and pitch a major hissy fit.

Here is how well it can work. There was this girl, a mere acquaintance, not a Queen—"Jennie," we'll call her. Jennie had a boyfriend she'd had for so long, the novelty had worn off, as will happen. So she had a few auxiliary boyfriends. She and one member of the auxiliary decided to take a week-long retreat, and she told the old-timer that she was going somewhere with a couple of girlfriends, namely me and my sister. Now, she did not ask us up front if we were willing to participate in this subterfuge, but we didn't think it would require any actual effort on our part, and so we reluctantly agreed to keep quiet. That was all we agreed to do.

He Ain't Nothin' But a Man

Well, as it turned out, the spot the two of them chose for their week of debauchery also happened to be the very place that my sister and I were going to be for a day. One day. Then we were moving on. Jennie said that we should meet them "for a drink." We foolishly agreed. At the appropriate hour she showed up with her camera and a whole bundle of film. We were then cajoled into going with her to any number of locations and putting on different clothes at each and posing for pictures with her at every stop—to make it look like we'd spent the week with her. It was pretty funny. So we did all that, and then we left and forgot all about it.

When Judy and I returned home on our appointed day, we learned that Jennie had come in a day earlier and gone to a movie with the auxiliary boyfriend, only to discover the old boyfriend sitting smack in the middle of the theater. Did she skulk out furtively? Did she make any attempt whatsoever at hiding? She most assuredly did not. Our Jennie, she marched herself right up to the unsuspecting chump and demanded (in explicit and extremely loud terms) just what in the hell he was doing in that movie. He was, as Elvis Costello would say, bobbing and squinting just like a nitwit, and dared to ask her the same thing, adding that he'd seen my boyfriend and learned that Judy and I weren't coming back until the *next* day.

He was sorry he asked that; he was very sorry, real quick-like. She gave him the full frontal attack, leading off with a resounding "You m——f——r!" and moving swiftly along with how she had had enough of me and Judy and was missing him so bad, she couldn't stand it, and so she just got on a plane and came back early to see his sorry ass; and not only was he not at home or at work to receive any of her "messages," she had to track him down in a f——ing movie in the middle of the dang day, and she really believed he must have done it on purpose; she knew he got all those "messages" and just ignored them and came in this movie to hide from her. And with that she burst into tears.

The guy who said that the best *de*fense is a good *off*ense was no dumbass.

7

The Five Men You Must Have

IN YOUR LIFE AT ALL TIMES

A very wise woman told us this once, and we really took it to heart: There are five different kinds of men that you must endeavor to have in your life at all times in order to have the equivalent of one completely satisfactory man. She explained that it is clearly not possible to find all the required attributes in one single man, and we should not expend needless energy by even looking for him—we'd be damn lucky to find the five separate men. Once in a blue moon, she told us, you might come across a man who has one and maybe a half of the attributes or maybe even two. Finding and maintaining convivial relationships with five very different men, all at the same time, in order to have one's basic needs met—it will not be easy, she cautioned. But it's at least possible. In her valued opinion, trying to live one's entire life without, say, dancing just because your man doesn't like to dance—well, you might be able to manage, but is this really something you want to spend the next fifty years doing, or in this case not doing?

The Basic Five are these: (1) a man who can fix things, (2) a man you can dance with, (3) a man who can pay for things, (4) a man you can talk to, and (5) a man to have great sex with. As I said, this is the rudimentary team you need to form, according to our sage adviser. Certainly other functions can be added to suit your more refined tastes, but with this starting lineup, you can at least avoid abject misery.

Oh, the allure of a Man Who Can Fix Things. Is there anything more appealing? Well, yes, I suppose there is, but you won't be able to think of it when the toilet is overflowing. When you've got a flat tire, or your bedroom doorknob falls off in your hand, or your new stereo is delivered in its various unconnected component parts, or your neighbors are threatening to barbecue your dog the next time he pops through the hole in your fence into their garden party—then the Man Who Can Fix Things will be the hottest fellow you've ever seen in your life. You will breathe harder when he gets the toolbox out of his trunk. He is your dream boy. But, you know, once the pieces are assembled and the wires all connected and the music is playing on your new stereo and you realize that he claps on one and two, Handy Andy's out. It's time for a Man You Can Dance With.

Dancing Jones comes to your side, and the two of you dance a hole in your shoes. But now the hunger's creeping up. Fred Astaire's younger brother would love to take you out to dinner, but he left his buy-one-get-one-free coupon at home, and so you either have to pay or cook. You'll have a lot more choices with the Man Who Can Pay for Things.

There are plenty of compliments we could pay to the Man Who Can Pay for Things, but by far and away the best one is that he can pay for things. And he will. Loves to. It's what he lives for; so for God's sake, humor him. Order everything on the menu, and he will smile indulgently. I don't know about you, but being smiled at indulgently is just way up there on my list of favorite stuff. I'm especially fond of being smiled at indulgently while being dandled on his knee. A good knee dandle is just hard to beat. And a good knee dandler is hard to find. Try and remember the last time you had a really first-rate knee dandle. Finding a Man Who Can Pay for Things and who will do so while smiling indulgently and providing excellent knee dandlage might tempt a girl to overlook the other four categories. This could prove to be disastrous.

Money and knee dandling are fine, but they do not a life

make. If you say to this man, for instance, "*Here's* something!" meaning "Listen to *this!*" and his initial response is "Where?"—you've got a problem. If you say to this man, in exasperation, "I ain't taking you *to raise!*" and he says, "Where's Ray's?"—he is a dullard of the first water and in grave danger of screwing up sack lunches, should any be in order. You cannot talk to this man, and you must have a Man You Can Talk To. One who will understand things without exhaustive explanations. High dramas cannot be played out with someone who always misses not only his cues but the punch line, too.

The Man You Can Talk To must be able to fully grasp the meaning of loyalty. Here's what is wanted: You call him and tell him you hate Joe, his best friend since the first grade and your lover. The only acceptable response from him is "I hate him, too. I hope he dies." He should not ask any questions—it is not necessary that he know *why* you hate Joe, only that you do. He should simply fall in line. Any embroidery he adds at this juncture about how much he hates Joe and how long he's hated him, while only pretending to like him for your sake, would be welcomed. If, for reasons best known to yourself, you find that five minutes later in the same conversation, you suddenly decide that Joe is, after all, the apple of your very eye, your darlin' sugar lump, he should immediately, without hesitation or question, say, "Joe is my very best friend, has been since the first grade, I love him like a brother, and seeing the two of you so happy together just tickles me to no end." Now, if you should decide after another brief interval that you were right in your first estimation of Joe—he's a lyin', cheatin' sack of shit—this man should not even miss a beat. "Hot-damn! I hate that guy!" should be his snappy rejoinder. He should be prepared to do this repeatedly and without end. This is the true test of loyalty. He should acknowledge, willingly and without prompting, that yours is the only dog in this hunt.

Now, let me see, what do we need now? By and by, I expect we'll be wanting to have sex and plenty of it. And that is something that is surely hard to find—the "plenty of it" part. I don't know about other places, but in the South we're big feeders. People come to your house, and you trot out more food just for lunch than they and all their kin can possibly eat in a month—all in the name of hospitality. The guest is expected to rave endlessly about the quantity and, of course, the quality of this feast. The hostess is expected to disparage the whole thing as absolutely pitiful: It was all she had time to prepare, and not even close to what all she *would* have prepared if she'd had an ounce of human decency and another thirty minutes or so. This little dance should be repeated frequently throughout the duration of the visit.

According to a story my father used to tell, my grandfather was the guest of the most acclaimed hostess in Attala County. You could drop by her house at any hour of the day or night with a school bus full of people, with no notice whatsoever, and she would lay out a spread that would feed and significantly raise the cholesterol level of the entire county. The table groaned with the sheer weight of all the food she had prepared for my grandfather, and so as to be polite and not hurt her feelings, he dutifully sampled all of it, in no small way. He ate and he ate and he ate. She waited graciously for him to begin the praise cycle. He never did. He just kept on eating. She waited as patiently as she could, and still he said nothing. The whole rhythm of the meal was being thrown off.

She tentatively began to make brief unsolicited sallies into the denial/disparage/denigrate cycle of the thing. "The beans were a little mushy, I thought." "And the biscuits were hard, weren't they?" "I just dried that chicken out, I'm always so afraid it'll be red at the bone, I just overdo it, I never could fry chicken like my mama." He would dutifully refute all her unwarranted and untrue statements as just that, but he would not follow up with the culturally appropriate and desperately sought hymns of praise for her food. She grew more distraught by the minute until finally she could stand it no more and she broke the cardinal rule of Southern hospitality: She just flat-out asked him if he liked the food. Being entirely cognizant the whole time of her horrendous discomfiture, he leaned back (back being the only direction he could lean, so engorged was his belly), gazed about the table at the ruins of the feast, and said, "Well, yes, it was pretty good—what there was of it." Knowing at last that she'd been had, she began beating him about the head and body with a wooden spoon.

This saying, "It was pretty good—what there was of it," became the accepted code in those parts for the highest possible praise for a meal. And here's the point I intended to make when I started all this: If something is really good, there is no such thing as too much of it. Indeed, there hardly ever is even *plenty* of it. This applies to food, and it most certainly applies to sex.

A congenial partner for sex is highly desirable, and although many partners may theoretically be available, don't kid yourself, missy. Mr. Congeniality is not likely to be waiting around every corner. No, ma'am. Finding him will probably involve more looking than finding. But suppose after exhaustive, not to mention exhausting, research, you do find him—whose glance starts the smolder, whose touch sets off the towering inferno. Now, what do you reckon the odds are that he's also a plumber, a fabulous dancer, or a really rich guy with an uncanny knack for conversation and excellent listening skills?

So as you can see, five is the absolute minimum number of men you can make do with. The great news is that four out of the five can be gay! As a matter of fact, it would be a plus if they were gay. Because then they'll not only carry out the functions of their position extremely well, you can also get fashion and makeup tips, not to mention get your house featured in *Better Homes and Gardens.* Gay men are fabulous, perfect for us in every way except one; but you have to be careful not to fall in love with them because there is just no changing their minds on that score. Believe me, if it could be done, I would have done it.

8

Boyfriends and Fiancés

GETTING THEM
AND GETTING OVER THEM

B oyfriend—any and all heterosexual male persons who buy you dinner, take you to movies, etc. We do not have physical contact of any kind with a "boyfriend."

Fiancé—any and all heterosexual male persons with whom you are currently having sex. Fiancé status does not have any bearing, real or implied, on the ultimate future, if any, of the relationship. Fiancés must be in constant compliance with both the Four-Hour Rule and the Twenty-Four-Hour Rule.

Boyfriends and Fiancés

It is just so important to understand the distinction between Boyfriends and Fiancés and keep it clear in your mind at all times. Do not be hasty about elevating someone into Fiancé status prematurely. A Boyfriend can have all manner of habits and characteristics that would clearly signal danger if he were upgraded to Fiancé but that would not be an impediment of any kind in a mere Boyfriend. Since all the Boyfriend will get to do is pay for stuff, he can be a hound from Hell and it won't matter one whit. You'll find that you can painlessly have lunch with just about anybody. And keep in mind, nobody ever murders a Boyfriend. Fiancés, now, are another matter altogether.

Here's an important point to remember: "Never" does not really mean "not ever"; it doesn't even mean "hardly ever." What it actually means is "whenever you feel like it, for whatever your reasons." The man of your choice should never be able to predict when the tide will turn in his favor. He should know definitely that it is a *favor*, one that you can bestow or withhold at your whim.

Let's just say, for the sake of discussion, you have been particular and selected a guy. And let's just say that, for reasons best known to yourself, you have decided at this particular time and space to have sex with him, or at least to allow him to have sex with you. He's your fiancé. Two rules apply.

The Four-Hour Rule. This means that before you make him the happiest man in the universe and cause the earth to move beneath him and blood to seep from his ears, he must spend at least four hours demonstrating to you exactly how overwhelmed he is at the prospect. This should include rafts of compliments about everything from your eyes/face/hair/outfit and legs to the unbearable sweetness of your disposition. There should also be gifts and refreshments.

The Twenty-Four-Hour Rule. Assuming that he has complied suitably with the Four-Hour Rule and you did, in fact, participate on some level—any level at all—in some sexual act with him, then it is absolutely mandatory that he be in full compliance with the Twenty-Four-Hour Rule. The Twenty-Four-Hour Rule states flatly that within (well within, if he has any sense and/or hopes for the future) the first twenty-four hours following said act of sex, he must telephone to repeat all of the pre-sex compliments that he paid you regarding your eyes/face/hair/outfit and legs, and the unbearable sweetness of your disposition, plus, he should have thought up at least fifteen minutes' worth of new and additional compliments about the act itself. These compliments should contain glowing references to the smallest efforts you might have made on his behalf.

Graphic compliments regarding specific body parts not included in the previous listing are also nice. As a general rule, he should keep in mind that women prefer that some body parts be praised for their amplitude, while others should be lauded for being the tiniest thing he ever saw. The latter would apply most especially to our butts, if we are white girls, and also our legs. White girls do not love to be told that they have "such pretty big legs." That is a black thing. If you tell a white girl that she has a butt like a little ole butterbean, she'll probably marry you. Tell that to a black girl, and she'll poke out that bottom lip so far, she'll trip on it and you'll never see her again.

Now, the Four-Hour Rule can certainly be waived at your complete discretion. If you've decided that he deserves a random act of kindness from the universe—or more important, that you do—and you greet him at the door wearing nothing but your biggest smile, that is certainly acceptable. But it does not exempt him from the Twenty-Four-Hour Rule. There are virtually no exemptions from this momentous decree; only death or prolonged coma are even considered. Failure to comply must result in his being cast into outer darkness for an extended period of time—certainly never less than forty-eight hours, although a longer sentence would be more effective. During his time in that outermost dim and murky realm, you should not acknowledge his existence on this planet. Should you eventually decide, in your boundless mercy, to allow him to emerge from darkness and resume his place in your life, he should find that the Four-Hour Rule has been extended somewhat, so he has ample opportunity to reassert his worthiness.

Just remember, as women, we are just like ice—they ain't no substitute, honey.

Tammy's Rule

Okay, so you are now in a relationship. How particular you've been will become apparent soon. One former Queen, Tammy, meanest little woman you ever saw, has one rule and one rule only, and it serves her well. Works like a charm, as it were. Tammy's rule is: *Treat 'em like shit and never give 'em any.* She swears if you do this, men will follow you around like dogs. She continues the canine comparison by reminding us of how much dogs love to chase cars; they are not, however, particularly interested in catching them. I've been watching her work this magic for about twenty years now. I've seen her make any number of grown men bawl like babies, using only venomous words, spoken through clenched teeth, accompanied by a mean and squinty-eyed look.

The next day, those suckers are sending flowers, buying jewelry, cooking dinner—happy as pigs in the sunshine that their precious Tammy is speaking kindly to them again. But she's never nice to them for too long a stretch.

We're admittedly dubious about the "never" part of Tammy's Rule. Our friend in Connecticut (who likes to call himself "the Duke" and sometimes Tom, even though his name is John) told us about a study that demonstrates that "never" may not always give the best results. This scientific investigation was conducted to determine why some men would rather play golf than just about anything. They did the research using (what else?) rats. It's fascinating that they would experiment with rats, as opposed to just asking a bunch of guys, "What's the deal with golf?" I figure there were at least two good reasons for it: (1) They got a federal grant to do the study if they used rats. (2) They discovered they could get a straight answer from the rats.

So what they did, of course, was put a bunch of rats in cages with food-releasing levers. (A lab rat's idea of Heaven must be a place with no food-releasing levers.) One group's levers would release food every single time the rats pressed them. The second group's levers never worked. I guess they all starved slap to death—big turnover in these rat studies. The third group met with success and failure in a completely random pattern. Sometimes they could pump away on the doohickey all day long and never get a bite. Then other times they could just look at the thing right, and big wads of food would come tumbling out. The first group was fairly bored with the process: A steady diet of immediate gratification apparently palls quickly. The second group was not only bored with endless failure; they were withering away to nothing. The third group, though, was fairly obsessed with its levers.

Then the lab guys cut off everybody's supply. Nobody's levers worked at all, ever. All the rats were now starving. The group that had been completely successful on each try gave up pretty quickly when the source dried up. They had taken it so for granted that they were unskilled in working for it and not interested in learning. The rats that *never* got any at all had already given up and were just lying around waiting to die. But that third bunch that had met with inexplicable success, they kept at it twenty-four hours a day, seven days a week. They had calluses on their little ratty hands from slapping that lever, just knowing that the next time was gonna be the charm.

I can see with total clarity how this explains men and golf addiction. Most guys are not great golfers. (This is the most charitable way we can put it.) But even the lousiest golfer will go out there on a given day and do something unbelievably great. He has no earthly idea how or why it happened, and so he'll just keep on trying to re-create the magic. It was, in fact, just a random act of kindness by the universe, but he'll pursue that fantasy to his death. If he *never* has any luck, however... well, we see a direct correlation to Tammy's Rule here.

Jay at the Desk

Okay. Worst case: All the rules have flown out the window, and you're madly in love with the guy. You've been eating shit, running rabbits, and howling at the moon—all of which clearly should be his job. He's been participating—whether fully or marginally doesn't matter—and you are completely around the bend. In your mind the china's picked out, the honeymoon planned, the children named, and then what happens? It's squirrel time. He has gone to that all-time favorite guy place—Outta Here. And you are what is commonly referred to as In a Hole. If you could find an actual hole, deep enough and dark enough, you would happily crawl off into it and sever all ties with life as you know it. Life is just bleak, and nothing, with the notable exception of food, holds any appeal for you. (The hole would need to be large enough to house a refrigerator and a microwave.) All you want to do is cry and eat.

But don't you do it. Snivel a little and have a fair-sized medicinal snack, and then get over it. Here's why. One of the Queens, Tammy, had a guy just absolutely rip her very heart out and use it to fix a flat, right before her very eyes. And she crawled through life for months and months and spent all kinds of money on therapists trying to figure out what happened (he dumped her), and why (he was a squirrel), and what she could do about it (not a damn thing). Then one day he called her again, out of the proverbial blue. And she felt... *nothing.* Shortly after that, as soon as she realized that she felt ...*nothing,* she got real excited. She felt really good. Now, all this happened while she was at work, naturally. If there's the slightest chance that a guy can turn you into an emotional wreck during the course of your normal nine-to-five, he will take it every time.

Well, as it happened, there was a young man who worked

in her building. A nice enough young man, although she didn't know him personally at all. His name was Jay, and he sat at the front desk. When she was relating the story to me of how the asshole had surfaced in an attempt to weasel back into her life and how she had lived and breathed and prayed, waiting for this very moment, dying to have him back, and when he finally called her to make all her dreams come true, she felt… *nothing*, she squealed delightedly into the phone, "Nothing. I felt NOTHING! He could have been Jay at the desk for all I cared!" And so "Jay at the Desk" became synonymous with being totally over somebody. They become Jay at the Desk.

Another Queen, Tammy, had a hideous relationship with a squirrel that lasted literally years. None of us thought we could survive it. It was a toss-up as to which was worse, when they were on or when they were off. It was just awful all the time. And then finally one day it really did end. No one knew why it was different this time, but everybody knew it was. Tammy took up permanent residence In the Hole. Chain-smoked. Took mood elevators that did little to differentiate her from a bug stuck on its back. Cried all the time. All the time. The swelling in her face never went down. She was just hoping he would come back. She was well along in that aspiration, when one day he approached her from the opposite end of a large parking lot, and he called out solicitously, "Hey! Tammy!" She smiled and waved and thought to herself, "Who is that fat guy hollering at me?" Not only had she not recognized him, she perceived him as "that fat guy." He had become Jay at the Desk. And the good news is, no matter how bad you feel, sooner or later they'll all become Jay at the Desk.

My friend Fran works in a building with its own employee dining room. Fran's had her share of ups and downs with men, and one of the ladies who works in the dining room has been there long enough to read the faces of the folks she serves. Fran came in one day, and the lady took one look at her and said, "Git another one." Fran was confused, since she had not spoken a word. "What?" The lady laid her hand on Fran's arm, looked her squarely in the eye, and said, "You don't have to say a word. It's a man, I know it is. Git another one. This one don't do right. Git another one." As my daddy used to say whenever he thought too much of a fuss was being made over something lost or broken, "They makin' them thangs ever' day."

So dispense with all the weeping and wailing. Let him be Jay at the Desk sooner rather than later. They're making men every day. Just get another one.

9

Men Who Love Us

AND THE INCREDIBLE LENGTHS TO WHICH THEY GO TO DEMONSTRATE THEIR LOVE

Many men give us money, as you may well imagine. Not us individually, you understand, but collectively—to support our efforts. Believe me, being a Sweet Potato Queen is no cheap deal. The outfits alone cost a fortune. And then, of course, we have to have new hair and accessories every year. Naturally we have corporate sponsors to whom we are deeply indebted, and they are, in fact, the only men we have ever loved. Our dear friend Skippy bought us all new fishnet stockings one year, the only stipulation being that he got to personally straighten all our seams. This was a win-win situation all the way around.

But there is one man who shall remain nameless, who really went to extraordinary lengths to prove his love for us. Naturally this man, who is a prominent and very successful man, would be proud and honored to be identified, to have his name bandied about in connection with us. Now, there's only one reason he's remaining anonymous. If I were to tell you who he is, every woman in this country would be trying to lure him away from us, and we intend to keep this one all to ourselves forever.

It was late in the afternoon of parade day, and the Queens were taking their only break from pleasing the crowds. We had gone into Hal & Mal's, previously identified as the official restaurant of the Sweet Potato Queens, chosen a table, and advised our doting waiter that we would be having everything fried on the menu, plenty of it and plenty quick. He scurried off.

Just as we were beginning to relax from the strain of making sixty or seventy thousand people happy, the cutest man we ever saw came over to our table. By way of introducing himself, he plopped down on the floor, on his back, and slid himself underneath our table, amongst all those legs and gold majorette boots. We all squealed girlishly and yanked him up, then situated him in a chair at our table. No other man in the whole establishment was invited to be seated in our presence. He was pretty pleased with himself.

After a bit, though, he obviously felt compelled to give us something of himself that could be acceptably presented to a large group of large women in a public place by a lone man. He calmly, with immense grace and dignity, unwrapped a single pat of butter, and removing his cap, he smashed it, the single pat of butter, on his totally bald head.

More girlish squeals and clapping. And so it went for the rest of the time we had together. Every few minutes another pat of butter would take its place on his dome. "Generations of men in my family have proven their love for their women in this way," he said. "Men with hair cannot do this." We assured him that men with hair are highly overrated in our opinion, and we, personally, would not give you two cents for a man with hair. He beamed with joy and applied more butter.

By this time we had consumed all the fried stuff we could stand, but there remained on the table a few french fries, a bit of a cheeseburger, and a couple of odd hot tamales. This, alas, also went on his head, a bit at a time. And so it was that his cap became a cornucopia of delight.

Now, if we can only get him to give us money.

Gifts ～ Fit and Unfit

Presents, too, are always welcomed by the Queens, although some items will not be well received. Take, for example, jewelry. It falls in one of those dangerous gray areas, but let us clarify that. *Expensive* jewelry is profoundly appreciated. Wildly expensive jewelry, quite naturally, would be wildly appreciated, and your basic good jewelry should not be ruled out for everyday gift-giving occasions. Cheap jewelry, however, is worse than no jewelry at all, and there are very few things in life that are worse than no jewelry at all. Any item of jewelry that contains pink or lavender stones that do not actually exist in nature itself is grounds for immediate dismissal. Antique estate jewelry is good. Gold nugget jewelry is bad. Anything available by the gross from a discount house is bad.

But guess what—you can spend big old wads of money on jewelry and still go wrong. One of the Queens, Tammy, received as a gift from one of her fiancés the worst-looking piece of jewelry any of us had ever seen. And it had cost him a bloody fortune. She could have bought a BMW with that amount of money. It was one of those giant gold coin pieces mounted in about a pound of gold, with big gold stems shooting out all the way around and about five pounds of diamonds stuck grotesquely on these stems. This monstrosity was suspended on the center of her chest by a gold chain that you could have moored a big-ass motorboat with. "Oh my God, you aren't gonna have to wear that hideous thing, are you?" She sadly said yeah, she had to because he was so proud of it. Picked it out all by himself, don't you know.

He wanted her to wear it all the time. She'd have on this fabulous Armani suit or something, and smack in the middle of it would be this *thing*, just hanging there. It was depressing, but Tammy was a good sport. She wore it day in and day out. Then one day, after it had been insured for a decent interval, it was stolen!

Now, it probably really had been stolen, and I'll go straight to Hell for even implying that Tammy would've flung that precious gift out her car window. She certainly has never admitted any such an act, but she has expressed the fond hope that the person who did find—my mistake, *steal*—her favorite necklace has profited from it handsomely. A sweet-spirited, forgiving girl by nature, our Tammy never could hold such a grudge.

Do not *ever* give a Queen a home appliance as a gift. Period. The end. Now, an exception can be made in the event she just happens to mention in passing that she wishes she had, say, a full Viking kitchen, and then she goes out of town for a few days; and when she comes back, her entire kitchen is renovated with fabulous Viking appliances. She will just be touched. On the other hand, if it is her birthday and you, all on your own, select, purchase, and present her with a Crock-Pot, well, you are over.

The Queens also do not want anything that can be described as "cute country." Talk about your oxymoron. And don't bring us any kind of wreath for our door unless it's

Christmas. Under no circumstances are you to buy us one of those home vacuum cleaner disguises that we first saw at crafts fairs but that are now appearing on the much-revered home shopping channels. These are not intended to transform a person or a thing into the guise of a vacuum cleaner, but rather to disguise the vacuum cleaner itself as something else—like a giant duck, cat, or doll. At a crafts fair you can buy one that will disguise your vacuum cleaner as a giant Mammy, but that is way too politically incorrect for the enlightened souls at the home shopping channels. Someday I hope to meet a person who actually owns a vacuum cleaner disguise that he or she personally bought on purpose. I want to know: Why don't they just keep their vacuum cleaner in the closet? Why would they want it sitting out in the middle of the living room looking like a four-foot-tall duck?

Is this present-day obsession with disguising everyday household items a purely Southern thing? My friend Allen Payne, who grew up in Philadelphia, Mississippi, and now lives in New York City, assures me that vacuum cleaner disguises are simply not seen in New York. He also swears you cannot buy a lacy phone book cover or a crocheted cover for that extra roll of toilet paper. Why does anyone feel the need to dress up a roll of toilet paper in a little frilly outfit and set it on the back of a commode? You can also buy tiny aprons to dress your two-liter bottles in. They look just like real cooks' aprons—the little loop around the neck, the pocket, the strings that tie in back—and they come in the most festive colors and patterns. So now, even though that empty bottle of Pepsi is only going to be there on the counter for a few hours, while it is there, it can be appropriately dressed.

I guess naked soft drink bottles in the kitchen and bar could be jarring to one's sensibilities. Maybe they should wear clothes until garbage time. There's probably some crafty individual, right at this very moment, creating appropriate burial attire for used toilet paper, empty Pepsi bottles, vintage phone books, and broken vacuum cleaners. The landfills would be so much more attractive if all the garbage were dressed up in little outfits. I bet Lady Bird Johnson would have a fit over this idea.

If, however, we should happen to mention to the Man du Jour that we are considering having our own Queenly selves disguised somewhat—or as we say, *altered*—in some fashion, his immediate and vehement reaction should alternate between swearing that we will only do such a thing over his dead body and begging us not to change a single thing about our most perfect selves—he cannot even bear to think of it. He should go to considerable lengths to convince us that the way the crepe of our eyelids actually hangs down far enough to distort our vision is adorable and that the way our chest is completely devoid of anything titlike—well, that's just the way he always dreamed tits would be. Whatever it is we have determined, after endless hours of scowling into the mirror, to have fixed—that should be his very favorite part of us.

I mean, you know you're a mess and something needs to be done and soon—you know this—but you don't want the man in your life to agree that you do, in fact, look like a dog-faced Al Capone. He should swear that any alteration to your perfection would be a shameful waste of good money, money that could better be spent buying you jewelry and Caribbean cruises. He should acquiesce only to please you. Then he should, of course, pay the doctor and smile indulgently as he writes that big ole check. After it's done, he should for a very brief time mourn the change; then he should forthwith endlessly extol your beauty. And he should never, *ever* mention the procedure again. Disparaging comments about your previous state will result in an immediate loss of playground privileges.

The Man We're All Looking For

There is this woman I know and love—I named my daughter after her, for crying out loud (my daughter's real name is Bailey; surely you didn't think I'd actually put "BoPeep" on the child's birth certificate?)—who has all the best men. If you are wondering why you can't find a good one, call Joan Bailey; she's got them all to herself, the bitch. She's married to one, she gave birth to another one, one is her brother, one is her son-in-law, and then on top of all that, she's got the Amazing JB. For years she'd been regaling me with tales of the Amazing

JB and producing all manner of obscene cards and letters allegedly sent by same—with return addresses like "Treasurer, PTL Ministry, Trust Me Lane, Big Lick, South Carolina."

Finally I could stand it no more. I demanded to be put on his mailing list, and thus I, too, became the pen pal of the Amazing JB. He and I, although total strangers to one another, began sending stuff through the mails that required the traditional plain brown wrapper (sequined jock straps, crotchless running shorts, personal pleasure devices disguised as vegetables, and the like). Joan and I would compare atrocities received several times each week. MoonPie and Joan's husband, Buster, were at times appalled by the trash sent to us, but they didn't see the trash we were sending out.

Well, starting one January, JB began threatening to come for a visit. Said he was gonna get on a Greyhound bus and come to Jackson in September. Every correspondence we received for the next nine months made reference to his coming to town on the 'Hound. In the spring he named September 23 as his arrival date, and we began getting several cards a day, ranting about his long-awaited arrival at the downtown 'Hound pound. This barrage continued for months. We were starting to get nervous.

On September 22 I received two cards, "See you tomorrow." Joan did, too. We didn't know whether to shit or go blind. All day we were on the phone: "Is he really coming?" Buster, who was obviously in on it through JB himself, swore to God it was true. At 9 P.M. on September 22, Joan got a phone call from some official-sounding guy saying he was the national president of Greyhound in Denver, Colorado, and he was just calling to confirm that the Amazing JB would, in fact, be arriving on the 12:15 bus tomorrow. (The thing is, JB is the kind of guy who could actually get the president of Greyhound to make such a call.) Joan hung up the phone, and Buster confirmed that the headquarters for Greyhound are actually in Denver. We were perplexed. See, if he was really coming, we wanted to dress up real trashy and go to the bus station to meet him. But then again, if he wasn't, then there we would be at the bus station in gold lamé shoes, for goodness sake.

Six A.M., September 23: Buster was leaving town. Joan gave him one last chance to tell the truth. "Look at me, Buster," she said. "If you lie to me about this, do not come home ever." Chuckling, Buster took a solemn vow that really and truly at 12:15 that day, a Greyhound bus would arrive in Jackson, and on board would be the Amazing JB, and "Y'all damn well better be there to meet him; he's coming all that way from North Carolina on a bus just to see you!"

We vacillated, but then we decided to take our chances. We met at 11:45 and went to the store to buy Tootsie Rolls to black out our teeth with. They didn't have any Tootsie Rolls! I went nuts. "What do you mean, you don't have any Tootsie Rolls? What the hell do you have in here? What are we supposed to put on our teeth?" The clerk was confounded. I bet they have Tootsie Rolls from now on, and everyone will have me to thank for it. I mean, really, whoever heard of a squat 'n' gobble–type store that doesn't carry Tootsie Rolls? Off schedule now, we raced to a nearby drugstore, which fortunately did have Tootsie Rolls. On to the bus station.

We parked right in front and proceeded to dress in the car. We didn't do as elaborate a job as we would have liked because we still didn't wholly believe JB would materialize. Joan put a big Tootsie Roll over her teeth, and BoPeep put on her tiara, which, because of her hairless condition at the time, had to be secured with surgical tape. I put on my "Barq's Root Beer with Metamucil" cap, my red sunglasses with the flashing lights, my T-shirt that reads, "Eat Me Raw at Fuddrucker's" (a gift from JB), and a liberal coating of Tootsie Rolls over my own front teeth. 'Peep at this time had no teeth, so she was set.

We pranced into the bus station like we had good sense. The bus arrived. A man alighted from the bus wearing a priest's robe, a baseball cap, and a button that said, "Drop your drawers and then I'm yours." He knelt, in the middle of the bus station, as if in prayer. *As if,* is right. This would be John Burress.

We whisked him off to lunch at the Mayflower Café, a great old, funky diner-type establishment in downtown Jackson. The Mayflower is a place to which we could go dressed as we were, Tootsie Rolls and all, and we would be given the exact same service as if we were dressed to the nines—surly. The customer service at the 'Flower is a sort of insider's joke. You go there your whole life, and it seems normal for the staff to be crabby. Sort of like your mom: She's *willing* to wait on your sorry ass while you just sit there, perfectly capable of doing if for yourself, but she's pissed off about it anyway.

The Mayflower also has one of the most bizarre rest rooms in the entire world. First you have to go through the kitchen, and if you think the wait staff is crabby—it's hot in the kitchen, and the cooks are having to slave over a stove in the heat while you just sit out front laughing and talking and eating in air-conditioned comfort. You walk a little faster through the kitchen. Next you have to go up a really steep, really narrow flight of stairs, unlit except for a single naked lightbulb hanging from a cord in the ceiling at the very top of the steps. It looks like the kind of place one would go to have an abortion with a coat hanger. It's the scariest place I've ever been. I only went once. After one trip up those stairs, I vowed my bladder would burst and flood the place before I'd go back again. I know lots of individuals who feel so strongly about it that they'll go out in the parking lot behind the place, rather than face the stairs, and seek relief behind parked cars. And these are not all guys I'm talking about here. We made JB go to the scary bathroom, and he was visibly shaken for some time.

Anyway, JB had shown up with presents—two huge matching duffel bags full of them. We sat in the back booth of the Mayflower in our outfits, shrieking with pleasure over each new trinket, gadget, or marital aid to come from our goodie bags. And then out of the blue—or bag, as it were—came this gorgeous string of pearls, obviously very real. Joan and I didn't know what to say about it. JB spoke up and said, "Those are for BoPeep." Well! Tell me this isn't the most wonderful man in the entire world, living or dead. Here is a guy who takes almost a full year setting up an elaborate joke for our amusement. He gets on a plane in Winston-Salem, flies to Jackson, takes a cab from the airport to a nearby hamlet so he can get on a Greyhound bus and arrive as promised on the bus. He's obviously devoted a great deal of time and energy assembling his outfit, not to mention these enormous goodie bags, and he's been up since four o'clock in the morning just anticipating it all. And he brings my baby pearls! I love this man. Make me laugh and buy me sparkly things, and I am yours.

JB is truly deserving of his title, Amazing. He told me that this bus trip was one of those things-that-you-think-about-and-talk-about-and-they-sound-great-but-you-somehow-never-do-them. He had a number of such plans, he said, some funny like this one and some serious, but starting right then, he was going to actually *do* one of them every ninety days. John Burress is so alive and so glad of it and so willing to do something about it. I wish there were a hundred of him, but there is only one. He is fit for a Queen.

10

Men Who Signal Danger

BE ON THE LOOKOUT
FOR THESE RED FLAGS

Experts tell us that all the warning signs of a bad relationship are there for us to see in the first ten minutes after meeting. I am here to testify to that, although it's never deterred me in the slightest. But perhaps my experience can benefit others who are more willing to pay attention.

Wild About Hairy

I have personally found hair to be a pretty fair index for future problem potential. Here are some examples—see if you can spot what the problem will be. Consider these first two guys, both of whom have what I would consider to be some of the world's best hair. Or rather they did have, until they started jacking with it.

Guy Number One had this really thick, slightly wavy, salt-and-pepper thing going—truly some of the best hair I've ever seen. Everywhere he went, people would comment favorably on his hair. Stylists would positively salivate over its texture and sheen. Not for any amount of money could any stylist anywhere duplicate those subtle shadings. His hair was one of those perfect flukes of nature. *Was* is the operative word here. He decided it looked "gray," and he got some yay-hoo to bleach it for him. So instead of white streaks that really looked more blond than white, he now has orange streaks through a gold background. It is the worst hair travesty I have ever witnessed. The stylist should have her license revoked for malpractice. From a distance now it looks like a football helmet—either Tennessee or Notre Dame, depending on the light. I was too undone over it to even make an attempt at being nice about it. He said he thought it made him look younger. I told him it made him look like an old guy with a bad dye job.

Guy Number Two is my erstwhile husband, MoonPie, who had a really nice, well-groomed coif for the first ten or so years I knew him. Then one day, out of the blue, he showed up with that new look that is so ridiculous looking. You've seen it.

It looks sort of like they put a bowl on the guy's head to cut it—almost no hair on the sides and back, shaved up, and then all this long, floppy stuff on the top. Totally undignified and nasty-looking, too. The Queens can't stand a guy, or a girl either, for that matter, with hair that's always flopping down in the face. So you've got all these guys who are constantly pushing their hair back, or even worse, they've learned how to *toss* it back, like a redneck girl in a boondocks bar.

I was not kind to MoonPie. For one thing I was once married to him; that relieves me of the normal societal burden of having to be nice to him. I might have made some effort except it was just such a shock. This guy is *always* dressed to the eyeteeth and groomed to perfection. I'm saying he wouldn't go buy a Sunday paper without a shower, shave, and ironed blue jeans. Stunning that we are no longer married. At any rate, the words just tumbled out before I knew it. Something like "What in the world have you done to your head? That's the worst-looking mess I've ever seen in my life! Who did this to your beautiful hair?" And I repeated things of this nature every single time I saw him for the next several weeks, to no avail. He actually seemed to be *pleased* with what greeted him in the mirror.

Finally I found the solution. A mutual friend of ours saw him at a function and reported that she had finally seen first-hand the new do that I had been ranting about, and she had the perfect description for it; but I had to swear I wouldn't tell him what she said. So I swore away and then promptly called him up and told him anyway. It was too good. She said he looked just like Moe in the Three Stooges. Let me say that he could not get to the barber—or in this case, *stylist*—quick enough, and that was the last we've seen of that mess.

We were all atwitter about the dye job and the Moe-do, and then one of our friends, Cozette, had a semiclose encounter with a guy who maybe had no hair at all. I say "maybe" because it was never determined for sure one way or the other, and the whole thing was just a trauma for her. See, she had met him at the Olympics in Atlanta. Cozette actually met quite a number of men there, from all over the world. Of course, she is the type (read: little, blond, big tits—enough said?) that men would notice from across a crowded stadium and walk across the backs of all 350,000 people who have the misfortune of being between him and her—just to be near her. The rest of us are the type that the same men would ask us would we mind moving down some so they can set their beer there.

So she met this guy at the Olympics, and when they met and he fell hopelessly in love with her, he had on a baseball cap. Now, this was not the guy from Sweden who owns the equivalent of, say, Merrill Lynch over there. And this is not the guy who lives in New York and is the most handsome man in this hemisphere. No, this was the other guy she met, the one who just sold his company, which wasn't Microsoft but a reasonable facsimile. Get the picture? If I had gone to the Olympics, I would've been damn lucky to catch the eye of the peanut guy if I was starving and waving hundred-dollar bills at him.

At any rate, post-Olympics, the baseball cap comes to Jackson to call, only he ain't wearing the cap. He's wearing, she's pretty sure, a rug. It was all she could think about over drinks and dinner. She felt her eyes irresistibly drawn to his head. She was mesmerized, as it were, by his hair, or rather what purported to be his hair, but she was pretty sure it had been *somebody else's* hair up until recently. She found herself positively obsessed with divining the truth—turning her head this way and that, trying to view it from the angle that would be most revealing. At one point she even tried to walk behind his chair and sort of bump into him, stumbling, thereby allowing her to grab hold of his head in order to steady herself—and still she couldn't be certain. The uncertainty plagued her. We raised the question of whether perhaps, just *perhaps*, it wasn't a rug after all but he'd actually grown that fine head of hair.

We don't understand the theory of toupees. We don't know one solitary female who would refuse to go out with a guy with no hair. On the other hand, nobody can take a man seriously who wears a wig. Or who perms his hair—can't you just see him sitting there in his little cape with all those tiny rollers in his hair? Wouldn't you get that mental picture at the most inopportune moments? And what about guys who color their hair? On the coloring issue it was a split vote among us as to who is more repugnant—the man who darkens his hair, the man who bleaches his hair, or the one who gets his hair frosted. (He would rank up there with the perm guy for sitting there with all those little hair sprigs pulled through that little cap.) Going to a beauty shop and getting your hair done is just not a guy thing. It's too creepy for words.

What are you supposed to think of a guy whose only gray hair on his head is about four white hairs on each temple, while the rest of it is a uniform shade of brown that does not naturally occur in living things among any of the various species that grow hair? And then he takes off his shirt (if you can stand to let him, knowing what you already know about his beauty shop habitudes), and you're confronted by a heavy thatch of snow white chest hair? Are you really expected to have no thoughts whatsoever about this incongruity?

Hairdos, coloring, perming, augmenting, and so on—all this is girl-type stuff. We're not interested in having any of our guys assume or usurp any of our girl-type activities. We find that we can't take them seriously as guys if they do these things. As a matter of fact, we don't like men to fuss with their hair at all. We can't respect a man who spends more time on his hairdo than we spend on ours. If he's paying all that attention to his hair, he's not paying nearly enough attention to us, and that's the rub.

Plastic Parts Won't Help

We believe this to be true: All people, including us, get better looking—or worse—the longer you know them, and it's got very little on earth to do with what actual physical attributes they possess. Some guys are gorgeous until they open their mouths, and then it is so over. By the same token, we know any number of men who are not only not classically handsome, they tend more toward plug ugly, but they are so smart and so funny and so charming and they pay so much attention to us that we think they are the most attractive men who ever lived.

This brings up the subject of plastic surgery. The rule is this: Women may alter any and all parts of their bodies repeatedly and forever. Men may not have any sort of plastic surgery whatsoever unless they've received third-degree burns over at least eighty-five percent of their anatomy. Implants masquerading as major muscle groups are unacceptable. If you're too big a weenie to work out and build some respectable pecs, you must go through life with the chest of a wren and everyone must know it. We know a guy who got calf implants, and now he wears shorts even in blizzards.

It cannot be emphasized often enough—if a man is paying too much attention to his own appearance, he is not paying nearly enough attention to ours. The only looks that are important are ours.

You Can't Put a Saddle on a Clothes Horse

This clothes angle with men is a tricky one to read. We're certainly not suggesting that you seek out men who wear cheap clothes. No, they don't even register on our radar. If a man wears cheap clothes, it's for one of two reasons—it's either a freewill choice (not a good sign) or he has no choice (also not a good sign). If he can afford whatever he likes and he likes cheap clothes, he will more than likely want you to wear them as well, and this, of course, is not an option. If he wears cheap clothes because they're all he can afford, we're certain that he's a very nice man with many wonderful qualities, but he can't afford you, dear, so don't toy with him; it isn't nice. It doesn't take long to ascertain whether he's truly cheap or just poor.

The man who wears expensive clothes is another matter altogether. We want him to look good, to complement us, naturally. However, the *appearance* of prosperity is not enough to make us happy. It is, in fact, just enough to make us mad. Not just angry-mad either; it can make a person crazy-mad. If you date this man, he will dress up in total-body Armani, take you to the finest restaurant, order everything on the menu, and belatedly discover that he left his wallet somewhere, although it doesn't matter where the wallet is—there ain't no money in it anyway. Nonetheless, you've been successfully manipulated into paying the tab. If you end up married to this man, you will wear the same clothes for ten years while he struggles to find his new sixty-dollar pair of socks in the dark, because he didn't pay the electric bill.

Living with Mom is the same kind of deal. It's imperative that you determine posthaste if he's living with her to take care of her or if she's living with him to take care of him. If Mom is paying all the bills and doing all the work, neither of them is likely to be very interested in bringing another woman into the mix, unless Mom needs some help taking care of the boy, in which case, all I can say is *"Run away! Run away!"* If he's taking care of Mom, it can be a very good sign. Just make damn sure you like Mom before you sign on for this gig; she could outlive you.

Men who look good but aren't will cost you heartaches and tears, pain and money. My daddy would say, in the vernacular of Attala County, Mississippi, "He needs to git further or smell better!"

I've never seen a man wear ill-fitting expensive clothes. Expensive clothes are never too tight or too short. I've also never seen a man in a pair of custom-tailored slacks wearing a tool belt. I think this cannot be coincidental. Explain this theory to me: A guy with a sixty-five-inch waist buys size thirty-two pants and simply fastens them below the big belly. Then, since guys are hipless, there's nothing to keep the pants up; and since his T-shirt won't cover the big belly either, we, the general public, are treated to a view of his belly from the front and his butt from the rear. Perhaps he's confused by all the articles in women's magazines declaring how much women love to look at men's asses. This is true, we do love to look at your butts, *but*—and I think I speak for all women here—we have to know you really well before we are remotely interested in looking at your *actual* butt. Until such time, we all prefer—in fact, we insist—that you keep it completely covered up. When we're ready to view your butt, we'll let you know, thank you.

Don't Sweat It

Some men sweat more than others. The ones we're talking about here sweat a lot. And let's just clarify for the record here that we're not opposed to this. One of the Queens, Tammy, used to date this really fabulous-looking guy with a major sweat problem. He was in perfect shape and quite the sight to behold when he ran, shirtless, in those itty-bitty running shorts outside in the Mississippi heat, which is formidable. The sweat would simply run off him in torrents. However, our Tammy liked it. Tammy always was a fan of water sports. She said he was just like a great big ole Slip 'n' Slide. Now, all this is to illustrate that sweat, and lots of it, is not necessarily bad. However, as you can plainly see from this fairly graphic illustration, we're only interested in a body-to-body transfer of sweat.

There are few things worse than the sensation of lying

down on a weight bench at the gym two seconds before you realize it's lathered in sweat from the inconsiderate asshole who just got up and didn't wipe down the bench before moving on. I hate him. I hope he dies and they bury him in that ratty-ass sweatshirt he's wearing that smells like he stopped on his way to the gym to roll in a dead squirrel. (If, in fact, I want to roll around in your sweat, trust me, I will communicate that to you privately.) A man who will do this is capable of God knows what-all in the personal hygiene department. Run away! Run away!

Adults Only on This Ride

The Queens are not interested in very young men. Even when we ourselves were very young, which we decidedly are no more, we preferred the charms of the older man. It's so odd that we are no longer numbered among the young. One minute, it seemed, we were young and cute, and the next thing we knew, we were all wedged up in front of a mirror pulling our faces up and back and wondering *how much it will cost to fix this.* We are one hundred percent in favor of fixing anything and everything by whatever means possible, and damn the expense.

I don't know when we crossed the line into ma'am-hood. I wasn't paying attention and never saw it coming. But now, whenever they hire new men in the weight room where we work out, they always call us "ma'am"—at least until we threaten to rip their tongues out and feed them to our cat. But then, seeing as how they are so all-fired young and energetic, we leave all our weights out for them to put away for us. We only want to be called "ma'am" if it is preceded with "wham bam" and a polite "thank you."

I don't feel like a ma'am. But apparently, I look like one, and that's worse. I totally agree with that guy who used to say, "It's better to look good than to feel good." However, I know I would *feel* a whole lot better if I didn't look like Whodunit. All of a sudden, when I take my hair down, I don't look like a flower child anymore. I look like Loretta Lynn. This is not a good look—for Loretta or me. Not to mention that there are big streaks of gray everywhere in my hair, but the last time I checked, Loretta was still using boot-black on hers.

When we go out dancing, usually at Hal & Mal's, the crazy old ladies up front who dance every dance are *us*. We do take much pride and satisfaction in the fact that, old and crazy as we are, at least we're out there. We haven't relegated ourselves exclusively to the TV. And according to our exhaustive research, we can still outdance and definitely outlast any twenty-one-year-old in the place. We find our youthful sisters and brothers to be either hopeless weenie people who cannot hang or limp-dick dead people who will not hang. We're proud to be of the generation who knows there used to be two Allman brothers and the first time we saw them play, they were playing warm-up for a band called Pacific Gas and Electric. Yes, we're old and getting more so all the time. Try to imagine how little we care.

And as I said, we've always preferred the company of older men. One of the main attractions here is that we will always be young and cute to old guys. This is a big plus. As a general rule, older men have more money to spend—on sparkly things—for *us*. Our ideal man at this point would be around seventy. His cataracts should be almost totally opaque. Remember that TV show *Moonlighting*, with Cybill Shepherd? They shot the whole show normally, but whenever the camera was on her, it had a cheesecloth filter over it. She always looked a little hazy and back-lit—therefore, fabulous. That's how we look to old men with cataracts. Once he's paid for our plastic surgery, we'll allow him to get his cataracts removed.

We also love to talk to men at least our own age or older so we have a common view of the world based on common experience—stuff to talk about. We've never understood the older guy–practically teenage girl thing. We've tried. We've belabored the point with our friend Randy, who, while in his forties, was dating a girl who was still in high school. He and his date—or, as we liked to call her, his "little friend"—would be late to everything. Randy would explain that she had band practice. When she was out of earshot, watching *Saved by the Bell* or something, we would berate him endlessly. We demanded to know what they could possibly talk about. When he wasn't immediately forthcoming with that info, we declared we could guess what they talked about, and we bet him a million dollars we'd be right, and we would know we'd hit it when we saw his face. "You talk about her hair and what happened on *The Young and the Restless*." Bingo. He had the decency to blush slightly.

There was much discussion about what a date would entail, since bars and some movies would be off limits. "Omigod! Randy! You have to go to the *mall!*" It took a while before he admitted it. Her dad had the presence of mind to voice some objections over this "relationship." The two of them—the dad and Randy, who graduated from high school the same year—met to discuss it man to man, over a beer. Somehow Randy convinced the dad that this was a good thing for his baby girl. We gave up. If it was okay with the dad, we figured, what the hell. We told him flat-out, though, that when summer rolled around and the Spice Girls were in concert, he was on his own; we were not going with them. Neither were we hosting a party to watch Nickelodeon's *Kids' Choice Awards Show*. We predicted that when she got old— like when she had all her molars—he would dump her. Which, of course, he did. It took a couple of years for him to realize that he missed his Friday nights at the high school football stadium.

Tammy had to double-date one night with such a couple. Tammy said she tried to be nice to the girl and include her in the conversation, but within a five-minute span the young-ster disavowed any knowledge of the Vietnam War and did not know who Jackie Onassis was. That was the end of the conversation for Tammy.

Here's the deal. People in their twenties and thirties should date each other, as should people in their forties and fifties. The only acceptable exception to this precept would be if *we* happen to be the younger women. Actually anything we do, anyone we want to go out with, is fine. We're only interested in passing judgment on the behavior of others. This is because we are so good at it, and we always want to excel.

11

Men Who May Need Killing

QUITE FRANKLY

It's sad—but even sadder, it's true—that a disproportionate number of men who you will be temporarily enraptured with throughout your lifetime will turn out, rather sooner than later, to warrant killing. It's just almost never a good idea to follow through—although, I swear, it seems like the only way to get rid of some of them. In our experience the more incorrigible the guy, the more deeply in love he is with us; and his tenacity is like that of one of those unrelenting Boston terriers that will bite the end of a rope and then you can swing the rope, dog and all, around over your head a hundred miles an hour all day long and the brute will never let go.

He will, however, never demonstrate that perseverance toward positive matters, such as paying the bills, giving up drugs and other women, or not farting loudly in movie theaters. He'll continue his objectionable behavior of whatever persuasion until such time that you, having reached your saturation point, declare closure. Then he'll pause in his objectionable behavior of choice long enough to attach himself to your ankles, sobbing, where he's prepared to remain until you forgive. It doesn't occur to him to go ahead on and find himself a woman who would count it her joy in life to support his sorry ass just to have the pleasure of his company night and day. He doesn't *want* a woman who wouldn't care how many other women he had because she has another half-dozen men on the string. If he finds a woman as cute as he is, that will steal his spotlight. If he finds one who's a bigger deadbeat than he is, who will feed them? No, he wants *you*, and you need to look out for yourself, or you'll be spending a lot of time hoping for zippity-do-dah, let me tell you.

Zippity-do-dah is our secret code for widowhood. Well, it's not exactly a secret anymore since one of the Queens told her husband about it. Shortly after she leaked this, he was at a men's church group meeting, and they were doing something sappy like standing around singing songs, and some poor oblivious guy requested that they sing "Zippity-do-dah," which they did, all except Tammy's husband, who went into hysterics and nearly had to be sedated. He kept ranting, "That's their *theme* song! Don't you know that?" What Tammy had revealed to him was this: Being a widow is way better than being a divorcée. It's better in every way. Financially, definitely. And it has to be far less damaging emotionally. Plus, everybody feels sorry for you and wants to help out. Nobody takes sides after a funeral the way they do with a divorce; there's only one side left standing. Widowhood is so much easier on the friend pool.

So what we like to envision is this: See the crowd at graveside. See the grieving widow in a smart black Ungaro suit, great shoes, heavily veiled but smashing hat. See the low-hanging clouds. See the mourners pay their last respects. See the solitary widow being helped into the ebony limo for her long ride back home alone. As the limo pulls away, see a break in the low, black clouds, allowing a single, brilliant shaft of sunlight to shine through. Behind the darkened windows of the limo, from deep behind the veils of the very smart hat, hear halting tones of the very small voice, "Zipp-i-ty doooo-dah...."

If you've waited a decent interval for him to expire, and it appears he won't, divorce is the only sensible avenue open to you. We've acknowledged the absolute folly of killing him your ownself, no matter how abundantly he deserves it. It will only result in further contrivance for you. As terribly inconvenient as divorce may be, it's not nearly so confining as capital murder. You can get an old friend to safely handle your divorce proceedings for free, *pro bono* as it were, but if you're on trial for your life, you're going to want to invest in the best defense available; and this is money that could be better spent on plastic surgery.

One of the Queens, Tammy, was going through a divorce a few years back, and her old high school sweetheart, a lawyer, bless his soul, handled the whole nasty business for her. He even paid her filing fee, the darlin' thing. When she got the first draft of the legal papers, we all congregated and read through them to be certain he had covered the important facets. We found him to be very thorough indeed. We were just reading along, one paragraph after another, just regular old d-i-v-o-r-c-e lingo, and then we came to a paragraph called "Optional." It read:

> It is agreed by and between the parties that the husband shall not procreate nor sire any further offspring by any means presently known or to become known in the future to man or science, to include but not limited to, normal intercourse, artificially manipulated mating, cloning or any other form of reproduction or sibilance thereof.

We're reading, and shouting, "Can we say this? Is this legal?" We read on:

To insure compliance with this, the parties agree the husband shall, within thirty days from the date hereof, admit himself into a qualified hospital or clinic of his choosing and undergo the proper and necessary surgical procedure and/or procedures to fully remove all genitalia from his person and erase all evidence of maleness from his waist down. The husband shall be under no compulsion, obligation or court order to "take this as a man." Within fifteen days of said surgery, the husband shall deliver to the wife all items removed from his body during said procedure and/or procedures, properly preserved, hermetically sealed and suitable for inspection, identification and exhibition.

Never mind that this was an affectionate hoax. Tammy's lawyer-friend belongs on the U.S. Supreme Court. We declare his words to be the ultimate final decree of divorce.

Is That a Wedding Ring in Your Pocket—or Are You Glad to See Me?

And then there are the Men with Nice Wives. I've found it hard to address this subject without my words having an *edge* to them, and so I gave up trying to eliminate the edge. The edge is there because so many of the Queens—indeed, we are but a microcosm of all womankind—have been Nice Wives, and man, does this piss me off. Of course, all the Queens were brought up as Aspiring Brides. As such we were counseled to obtain our teaching certificates so that in case we married football coaches, we'd be able to teach when their coaching careers were ended. For the same reason it was also acceptable to become a nurse. You could be a nurse or a teacher, but only if you *had* to work because your husband turned out to be a worthless piece of shit, but even if he did, he was still your husband for life, the king of you, and you were damned lucky to have him.

And so the young girl grew up to be the Nice Wife by doing everything her family and husband told her to do. She has been faithful and true, a cameo of abject perfection. She has borne and brought up children, often with exceedingly little help from the other parent. She has kept herself and her home in good working order. Meanwhile her husband is at a bar trying to pick up Bambi, and by way of explaining that white circle on his left hand where a wedding ring obviously resides most of the time, he says that, yes, he's married—*miserably so*—but he can't do anything about it because his wife has never done anything wrong; she is a very nice person! Somehow, in some convoluted way, it was not as infuriating when they used to say they were not understood at home, or they were married to the ditch witch but couldn't leave because of the children. (Speaking of whom, don't you know the kids would be proud of Dad now?)

It was just this sort of behavior that caused the Queens to search the Scriptures for guidance. After much deliberation we think we've come up with the first correct interpretation in around two thousand years. Remember that line that says, "It is better to marry than to burn"? Well, after centuries of theologians, most of them men, screwing around with it, the meaning got garbled. The true meaning is just exactly what it says: Being married is better than being set on fire. But they didn't say how *much* better; and from our own experience, it might not be such a clear-cut choice.

One of the Queens, Tammy, in the throes of divorce proceedings, sought advice from a close friend, Shirley. Shirley looked at Tammy with compassion and said to her, "You know, Tammy, if your husband was living according to the Scriptures, ya'll wouldn't be in this mess." Tammy said she didn't know what that meant. Shirley explained, "Well, the church folks just love to spout all that about wives submitting to their husbands. First of all, that presumes that the husband has some sense and perhaps more than an ounce of human decency. But the main thing they leave out is that the husband is supposed to be as Christ was to the Church." Tammy was still confused. "Christ died for the Church," Shirley explained. She went on to say that if this man was willing to put you absolutely first in every single decision he ever had to make, the whole matter was a guaranteed success. "Yes, I see your point," Tammy exclaimed. "If he would *die*, we wouldn't have to suffer through this awful divorce!" Shirley looked for an instant like the little boy whose bread was stolen by the chicken, and then she collapsed laughing. We do so love our sisters whose spirituality does not eclipse their sense of humor.

Anyway, the next time a Man with a Nice Wife tries to hit on you, promise me that you'll make a scene large and loud enough to alert all other women in the vicinity to his location. Try to involve as many of them as you can in the scene; a cast of thousands would be excellent. If he could later be found, bound hand and foot with women's panties, with a big red A indelibly painted on his forehead, wouldn't that just be gravy?

I think I kept most of the edge out, don't you?

No Peace for the Wicked

I spent a splendid weekend in Pittsburgh with a man who seemed too good to be true, and as it turned out, he *was*—but I get ahead of myself. I'll spare you the details of the fabulous weekend, as you'd no doubt throw up from sheer envy. Things deteriorated somewhat rapidly upon my arrival home, which I guess is to be expected. Never, however, could I have anticipated the particular turn that events would take within a few short hours.

I was exhausted. Being adored just flat wears me out. You?

Being waited on hand and foot for days is taxing. Got home to Mississippi by 9:30 P.M. In bed by ten, asleep by 10:03, with my daughter, BoPeep, beside me. I'd had about six hours' sleep the whole weekend, so being awakened at 2:30 A.M. was not exactly what I had in mind. Nonetheless, promptly at 2:30 A.M., I heard a noise. A very small noise: *ch-ch-ch-ch-ch*...It sounded exactly like my mother shuffling down the hall. (She's been enjoying ill health for the last year or so and lives with me and 'Peep.) Poststroke, Mama never picks up her feet when she walks. It's like living with Tim Conway's little old man character; I hear her coming for ten minutes before she gets there—drives me up the wall. So it's 2:30 A.M., and I was getting this *ch-ch-ch-ch* business. There were no lights on. I thought, not only is she up wandering around the house, she's also completely lost her mind trying to navigate in total darkness when she can hardly do so in broad daylight.

"Mother?" I call out. Again, "Mother!" No answer. I fling off the covers and stomp out into the hall, turning on lights everywhere. The hall is empty, and there's no sign of Mother. Her bedroom door is shut, and not a sound emanates from within. I crawl back in bed, putting my glasses on the night table. Only I miss the table and I hear them fall to the floor behind the table. I decide to worry about them later. I try to get back to sleep.

Again, the *ch-ch-ch-ch* noise. I'm livid, at what I don't know. I roll over to turn on the bedside lamp so I can begin the hunt for my glasses. On their own my eyeballs could be considered purely ornamental. I cannot see jack without major optical assistance. I'm not at all expecting to look down and see, sticking out from under the side of my bed, no more than a foot and a half from my very face, a long, hairless tail attached to a round, gray, furry behind. Having spent the last forty-five years trying to grow up in Mississippi, I know, instantaneously and beyond any shadow of a doubt, that tail and behind belong to a full-grown possum. Geezloueez! There's a possum under my bed! All I could say out loud was, "Oh!" but I said it real loud and over and over, with profound feeling. I can tell you, I was *completely* surprised.

I briefly contemplated calling The Man in Pittsburgh, thinking how interesting this would be to him at 2:30 A.M. since I bet this almost never happens in Pittsburgh because (a) I don't think they have possums up there to begin with and (b) if they do, they probably call them opossums and even pronounce the o, which everybody knows is silent and so why bother putting it in there? But I thought better of it and mustered the nerve to retrieve my glasses, which had landed approximately three inches from the nose of the possum. I sat there, on the edge of my bed, gazing at that possum butt and asking myself what in the samhill was I gonna do about this possum under my bed?

Everyone I've told this story to has butted in at this juncture, if not before, and wanted to know how the possum got in the house to begin with. I explained, as patiently as they deserved, that at 2:30 A.M. when you wake up and discover a full-grown possum under your bed, you aren't particularly interested in how he got in. You are, however, vitally interested in how he's going to get out.

Okay. I've got to have a plan. So I get up and go off in search of materials for constructing a possum trap. What would my daddy do? He would know, without the slightest hesitation, what to do when you wake up at 2:30 A.M. and find a possum under your bed. Daddy picked a fine time to be dead for fifteen years. Well, I'm nothing if not his daughter, I say to myself. I'll instinctively know how to deal with this situation. And so I'm led by some intuition into the kitchen—to the garbage, to be precise. (That possums love garbage is an irrefutable truth.) I select a suitably aged chicken package, containing some nicely ripened chicken skin and fat—manna from Heaven, if you happen to be a possum. I grab a large empty liquor box with a sturdy lid. Now hideously wide-awake, I return to my bedroom. I set the box in my bathroom, the delicate scent of the rotten chicken skin already permeating the air and, I hope, delighting my rodent roommate. I get back in bed and wait.

I have to do this in total darkness. Possums are nocturnal, and they don't like it when you turn the lights on. So I'm pretty happy. Just home after playing Queen for a Day all weekend. I'm trying to sleep a little so I can resume my real life as Mom to half the free world tomorrow, but instead of sleeping, I'm sitting bolt upright in the dark waiting for the possum under my bed to make a move on the chicken skin. Along about now I start to see the humor in all this. Now I'm sitting there, and I'm laughing fit to kill. This is too good, I'm thinking. I'm going to phone somebody. But who?

When it comes to calling somebody at 3 A.M., to report the presence of a possum under your bed, however, you are working from a very short list. I rule out The Man. I'm crazy about him but not certain that our relationship has progressed to the point that he's on my 3 A.M. Possum Report List. I think you probably have to be at least engaged for that. I decide that my sister, Judy, who lives in New Orleans, would probably want to hear about the possum situation.

I turn on the light momentarily to dial her number; then I perform a quick possum check. Still there, not a hair out of place. I get her voice mail. I'm talking really low to avoid awakening the slumbering BoPeep beside me, who is still blissfully ignorant of the fact that we have a possum under our bed. I swear, I barely spoke above a whisper, but somehow my voice reached into her sleeping brain. She catapulted straight up and began to shriek loudly, in staccato, "GET-IT-OUT-GET-IT-OUT-GET-IT-OUT!" And with that she fell back on her pillow, apparently still asleep. She lay still for a few moments and then sat up again, demanding to know if she had dreamed it, or was there in fact a possum under our bed? I've made a rigorous policy of honesty in her upbringing, and I could make no exceptions now. She demanded to know what I planned to do about it. I told her about the trap. She was dubious.

"Why don't you call Dad?" she asked. *"Dad?"* I can't convey to you the scathe in my tone as I repeated that word to her. "Dad? Darlin', Dad grew up in *north* Jackson, and I can just tell you, he doesn't know squat about a possum under the bed." MoonPie had lived practically forty years, all of them in Mississippi, before he accidentally stepped on a slug with his bare foot for the first time in his life. He let out a scream that was so loud, so piercing, and so prolonged that, hearing it from the back of the house as I did, I could only assume that a panther had bitten off his arm and was devouring it before his very eyes. He flew past me—if a large, grown man hopping on one foot and squealing could be said to fly—toward the shower. I fell on the floor in helpless guffaws. Who, born and bred in the South, doesn't know that you cannot wash off a smashed slug? I'll tell you who: MoonPie, that's who. He wanted to go to the MinorMed and have his foot amputated. From this knowledge I judged, and I think accurately so, that he would be utterly worthless to us at this time.

'Peep announced that she couldn't remain long in a dark room with a possum, and so off she went to the kitchen. On her way there she made a discovery. "There's possum poop on the dining room rug!" she shouted down from the hall. Well, now, that mobilized me. I hadn't considered the possibility of possum poop. Being a lot more familiar than I'd care to be with the offal of kitty cats, I could only imagine what the effect would be if this possum had a full *bladder.* I would probably have to burn the house down to get rid of the smell. Action was called for, and I was the only one on call. As I've always told BoPeep in times of crisis, "I can handle this and I will handle this because *I* am the great and powerful *mother!*"

I turned on the light and checked out the possum. Sound asleep he was, sawing big ole possum logs, right there under my bed. Not the slightest bit hungry, it would seem. That did it. I sprang up and got my great-great-granddaddy's walking cane that he'd carved by hand from a sassafras tree. I poked that possum with it until he woke up. I proceeded to try to herd him into my bathroom, hoping he wouldn't move farther up under the bed. He ran under the bench at the foot of my bed. I was down on all fours, nose to nose with this thing, jabbing at it with my cane, cussing all the while. I don't know if he was scared of me, my stick, or my profanity, but he ran into the bathroom. I followed him and slammed the door. I was now sealed off, alone, with the possum. I sprang into the bathtub, where I could reach him with my stick and prod him out into my exercise room. This having succeeded, it was simple enough to climb over the NordicTrack and onto a ledge, push open the door to the outside, and secure freedom for the possum.

A little while later I was on the walking track at the Y with

Gail. I told her of my weekend as the Queen of Pittsburgh and then about the possum. She concluded there was a moral to it all. "That's all well and good for you to run off up there to Pittsburgh and carry on with that handsome man, little missy, just so you remember that when you get back where you belong, there's gonna be a possum under your bed!"

As it turned out, it was a portent of things to come as well. The whole Pittsburgh relationship went from magical to mythical pretty much in one histrionic swoop. What seemed one minute to be a rapidly developing mutual admiration turned swiftly into something else altogether. After many multihour phone conversations, flowers, plane tickets—all of which indicated a certain level of interest—The Man suddenly said to me, "I am not interested in pursuing a relationship with you at this time." I said, "Excuse me?" And he said it again: "I am not interested...in pursuing a relationship...*with you*...at this time." I was particularly struck by his emphasis on the words "*with you*," clearly suggesting that a relationship with anybody else on God's planet would be given thoughtful consideration. *Nonplussed* pretty much sums up my feelings on the thing.

Of course, I immediately shared this information with my fellow Queens, who had been following the whole involvement quite closely, as you might imagine. All of them insisted that I had either misunderstood him or just blatantly twisted some innocent statement into something sinister. And so I repeated, for each of them in turn, the exact words, swearing on a stack of the holy items of their choosing that these were his precise words: "I am not interested…in pursuing a relationship…with you…at this time." They were just as taken with the "with you" part as I was and repeated his words to me frequently, as an aside to whatever we might be discussing at the moment, which had quickly ceased to be *him*. They forgot all about The Man from Pittsburgh but retained his parting words as some sort of mantra.

The big surprise came a month or so later when I heard from him again. He called my house, and my mother told him where I was, which happened to be a Queens' gathering at Tammy's house; he called me there. I answered the phone but failed to recognize his voice, and he apparently didn't recognize mine either. I handed the phone to Tammy. She said, in earshot of all the Queens, "Oh! Hi [his name here]! Yes, she's right here," and handed the phone to me. All the Queens shouted in unison, "We are…not interested…in pursuing a relationship…*with you*…at this time!"

He was calling because his latest very young thing had just dumped him unceremoniously, and he wanted to get on a plane at that precise moment and fly down for me to make him feel better, carefully adding that he was still "not interested…" This was what we call your slap in the face with a wet squirrel. I was so flabbergasted, I had to ask questions to be sure I was hearing what I was hearing. "You're telling me that this little girl hurt your ego so bad that you don't think you can survive it and you want to get on a plane and fly down here and you want me to drive all the way out to the airport at midnight to get you, whisk you off somewhere, and knock myself out consoling you for a day or so, and then you want to fly out of here and forget the whole thing? Is that what you're asking me to do?" He indicated that, yes, that was pretty much what he had in mind, did it sound okay to me? He was deadass serious. I replied that it certainly was tempting, but I didn't think I would be "interested at this time."

I walked back into the room with all the Queens, who, of course, were about to have a stroke wanting to know what he wanted. Once again none of them would believe me when I told them. "You are lying!" was their reaction. They all wanted me to call him back and tell him I'd reconsidered and I'd be happy to help him out and then not go to the airport to get him and, when he called, say, "I am not interested..." A lengthy discussion ensued at this point as to whether he just had brass balls or whether I did, in fact, have *chump* tattooed on my forehead and we had just never noticed it before.

I really must take some of the blame for this debacle. I've readily confessed that more often than not I'll see those red flags flapping in the breeze at first glance and willfully ignore them, plunging headlong into sorrow. In this particular case I'd blithely overlooked at least two sure signs that this was a man who might need killing: I had been duly apprised of his predilection for girls much younger, and I had personally observed the unmistakable tint of Grecian Formula. The words "I told you so," while so gratifying in application to others, are a serious irritant when directed at oneself. I'm curious. Wonder what FedEx would charge to deliver a live possum to Pittsburgh?

My senseless disregard in this instance of the red flags, and the consequences that followed, eventually reminded me, however, of pithy counsel from that wise old granddaddy of mine. He would look off thoughtfully and declare, "As you walk down life's pathway, you may chance upon a turd—don't kick it!"

12

What to Eat When Tragedy Strikes

OR JUST FOR ENTERTAINMENT

All tragedy is relative, of course. It could be anything from a car or plumbing failure to the death of the only woman in the world who has ever been able to give you a really great haircut. If you're in any way upset by something—it's a tragedy. A tragedy demands food, and lots of it. We Queens try to include items from all four major food groups— sweet, salty, fried, and au gratin. Balance is very important to us. You'll also want to have friends on hand for the tragedy-thwarting feast. Under no

What to Eat When Tragedy Strikes

circumstances, however, should you invite any of the assholes who refuse to acknowledge the depths of your misery. They can stay home and fill up on water for all we care.

Chocolate is the main staple of sedative food—the undisputed queen of all the comfort foods. I know this in my deepest heart. I frankly don't understand how people who are genuinely allergic to chocolate manage to put one foot in front of the other, day after day; I'd have to throw myself in front of a bus. I thrive on chocolate. My system requires an abundance of it every day, just to function normally.

CHOCOLATE STUFF

The Sweet Potato Queens' drug of choice is clearly my famous Chocolate Stuff. I got the recipe from my mother, who called it something like "fudge pudding." None of my friends could remember the name, however; they'd simply beg me to make them "some of that chocolate stuff." The biggest problem with the recipe is that it doesn't make very much. I'd recommend that you automatically double the ingredients. Doubled, it will make three pans. This has proven to be just enough.

Unfortunately it has to bake 40 to 50 minutes, which is a helluva long time when you're suffering. Good news: It's really just as fine—some factions argue *better*—eaten raw as fully cooked! We've been known to eat entire batches of it right out of the mixing bowl, skipping the baking altogether. Usually we're content with leaving copious amounts of the precious goo in the bowl and sticking our faces into the bowl while the oven works its magic on the major portion. When you make your personal judgment call, keep in mind that the recipe contains eggs, at this point raw, and you may be risking your very life in pursuit of instant gratification.

I've reduced the amount of flour by half and cooked it in the microwave for just eight and a half minutes, but you sacrifice texture this way, and I don't recommend it. One of the most important qualities of Chocolate Stuff is its unique texture: really gooey on the bottom and sort of chewy, crunchy on the top. Nuts are optional. We take our desire for nuts by spells, and this carries over into many aspects of our lives.

I'll tell you how to make my Chocolate Stuff, but your best option is to kiss my ass six ways to Sunday and get *me* to make it for you, because it's always better when I make it myself. I don't know why, I swear to God. The recipe I will give you does not omit any ingredients or instructions to sabotage your efforts. It just seems to know me, and it performs better in my hands. I even make it better than my mother does, and it was her recipe to start with.

Here's the deal: Beat two eggs with a cup of sugar and $1/2$ cup of flour. Add $1/4$ teaspoon of salt. In the microwave melt together one stick of real butter (I never use unsalted; I think it tastes flat) and 2 fairly heaping tablespoons of Hershey's cocoa. Get regular Hershey's in the dark brown box—anything else is different and will screw it up. Dump the butter-cocoa mixture into the other things, and stir it up good. Then add a running-over teaspoon of vanilla. I use real vanilla, but the grocery store kind won't ruin it. Stir that up, too. If you decide to go for nuts, use a whole bunch of pecans, chopped up fine.

Pour the Stuff into a greased loaf pan, set the loaf pan in a pan of water, and stick the whole business in the oven set at about 300 degrees. Depending on how your oven cooks, it needs to stay in there for 40 to 50 minutes. You can reach in there and tap on the top of it at 40 minutes. If it seems crunchy, I'd take it out. You can't really undercook it, since it's good raw, but you don't want to overcook it and lose the gooey bottom so crucial to the whole texture experience.

Trust me. This will be the best thing that has happened to you in a very long time, possibly ever. From now on, for as long as you live, just the simple act of getting out the bowl to make Chocolate Stuff will have an incredibly assuaging effect on your psyche. I can say, without fear of contradiction, there is virtually *nothing*, not one situation, that can't be faced with calm and grace and serenity if you have Chocolate Stuff. You can eat it and feel better *fast*, and when it wears off, you can just make another batch. Believe me, in no time at all, you'll be grinning like a mule eating briars.

The Queens have found what we think is a very effective eating pattern. *Sweet and salty.* For us this combination works equally well whether we're eating simply for recreation or if we're engaged in your true therapeutic wolfing. In our exhaustive testing of all the programs suggested in this book, we found that if we had sufficient quantities of satisfactory sweet and salty foods, we could eat for approximately seventy-two hours straight, with maybe the odd nap thrown in here and there. And you can appreciate, I'm sure, that there's healing value in this. The concept is that when you've sufficiently met your body and soul's requirement for sweet foods, your salty needs are practically screaming for attention. By the time you've gratified the salty, you'll be happily ready for sweet again. We're particularly fond of regular Ruffles and the original version of Fritos for some quick and effortless salty foods.

ARMADILLO DIP

Sometimes a life event is just too catastrophic for quick and effortless remedies. You'll need Armadillo Dip to go with those Fritos. New Allison gave us this recipe, for which we're eternally grateful, and as a token of our gratitude, we've allowed her to be a Sweet Potato Queen Wannabe. (New Allison is called New, by the way, because we already had an Allison. So when this one appeared, we had to have New Allison and Old Allison. If that wasn't enough confusion, we then got yet another Allison Wannabe. Since she's at least twenty years younger than the youngest one of us, we call her Baby Allison. We aren't currently accepting any further friends by this name.)

What to Eat When Tragedy Strikes

When New Allison introduced us to Armadillo Dip, being more fat-conscious than any of the rest of us are willing even to think about, she made it with ground turkey. To say the Queens are fat-*un*conscious would not be accurate at all; we're actually fat-obsessed, always seeking to increase the number of fat grams we can cram into any meal. As soon as New Allison moved to Chicago, we dropped the ground turkey and went for ground chuck.

You brown a pound or so of ground chuck. Pour off the grease; this is done purely for the consistency of the dip and should in no way be construed as a fat-saving measure. Dump in a bunch of taco seasoning, hot picante sauce, and hot Cheez Whiz. It's like a fancy Rotel tomato-cheese dip, a staple at all Southern gatherings—only hotter and more fattening. Armadillo Dip is great on Fritos and Tostitos, as long as they aren't the baked kind, which we're against.

NEW ALLISON'S MAMBO MARGARITAS

Occasionally, in order to feel adequately soothed and mollified, you're going to need some alcohol. The Queens are partial to margaritas, and New Allison's are hard to beat. You may think these sound weird, if not awful, but I promise it will become your favorite margarita recipe. You pour in one big can of frozen limeade; that's 12 ounces. Then add one bottle of Corona beer, 12 ounces of 7-Up (never Sprite), and 12 ounces of really good tequila. Don't attempt to mix this in a blender. We've all done it, trying to make them frozen, and blown the top of the blender and sprayed this sticky mess everywhere. (You'd think that would be so obvious, wouldn't you, what with the beer and the 7-Up?) A brisk stir in a fair-sized pitcher is the way to go.

FAT MAMA'S KNOCK YOU NAKED MARGARITAS

When we want our margaritas frozen or we're too lazy to mix up New Allison's, we have another plan: Fat Mama's Knock You Naked Margarita Mix. Tammy, who owns our favorite gourmet store in the entire world, called me one night and said she had a new product she was thinking about stocking, but we needed to test it first. Always willing to consume about anything in the name of research, I said, "Bring it over!" She arrived with two tiny bottles of Fat Mama's Mix and proposed that we commence the test. I said fine, but each of these cute little bottles makes 48 ounces. If we tested that much, we'd be sure to fail. We mixed up one bottle and found that 48 ounces was just exactly the right amount for the two of us, thirsty as we were and all. And I must say, the forty-eighth ounce was every bit as tasty as the first one. Plus, we *love* the name. We find that just saying the name makes us feel festive, which is, of course, a favorite Queenly feeling. Fat Mama's is made right here in Mississippi, and you can order it, no matter where you happen to live, simply by calling The Everyday Gourmet, a Queen-owned and -operated establishment. Call 1-800-898-

0122, and Tammy will be so happy to send you some of your very own.

ABSOLUT FREDO

Sometimes the Queens like to get all buffed up and go out among the grown-ups. Our favorite venue for acting grown-up is an Italian restaurant in Jackson called Bravo! We prefer to have martinis here—nothing makes you feel more grown-up than a martini—but we hate the regular kind. When Jeff Good, the proprietor of Bravo!, served us the Absolut Fredo, our lives took a couple of turns. It instantly became our favorite adult libation. Nobody else makes the Fredo in town, so we persuaded Jeff to disclose the ingredients, just in case we needed to feel grown-up somewhere else. Here they are: three parts Absolut Kurant, one part Triple Sec, and one part Rose's lime juice, all this shaken over ice and served exquisitely in a chilled martini glass. We've been unsuccessful in duplicating this drink at home. We whipped up a batch of them for watching the last Miss Mississippi pageant on TV, and they were singularly potent. Jeff didn't indicate what size the parts should be, and so we surmised them to be cup-sized. They were tasty, indeed, but we had trouble sitting up after just one.

OH, GOD!

We like to augment our sweet supply sometimes with fare that's not made with chocolate. One of our favorite supplemental sweets is a chocolate caramel pie that's come to be called "Oh, God!" I'm sure it originally had another name, but every single person, without exception, who's ever tasted this luscious concoction for the first time has exclaimed, "Oh, God!" It doesn't come out clear like that; it sounds all moany and, frankly, sexual—"*Oh-h-h-h! Gaw-w-w-wd!*"—clearly indicating extreme pleasure. There is absolutely no way to cram any more fat into a single food item. I got the recipe from my mother's friend Estelle, who is so sweet, you want to squeeze her guts out every time you see her. She has this hug-eliciting quality and comes up with recipes like this one.

First you make a pie crust, with 1 1/2 cups of flour, a stick of butter, and 1 cup of finely chopped pecans. You mash all that into a couple of pie plates and bake it for 10 minutes or so, at around 350 degrees, until they get tan. Then, in a pretty big bowl, mix together—this is so fattening, I can't even write it with a straight face—8 ounces of cream cheese, a can of Eagle Brand Sweetened Condensed Milk, and 16 ounces of Cool Whip—my three favorite ingredients. Pour this mixture into the tan pie crusts.

Meanwhile, mix together 7 ounces of coconut, a half stick of melted butter, and a cup of chopped pecans, and spread it all out on a cookie sheet and toast it. You'll have to really watch it and stir it a lot, or the coconut will burn slap up. Spread the toasted coconut combo on top of the pies. Then take a 12-ounce jar of caramel sauce, and pour it over the pies.

That is it. Freeze them for a little while before you try to cut them, or you can just sit down in the middle of the floor with a pie and a spoon and have at it—our preferred mode of serving.

COME BACK SAUCE

We've figured out why so many people in the world have eating disorders. Therapeutic eating works! I don't care what's happened, a caramel-turtle-nut-fudge sundae the size of my head from our favorite ice cream parlor, Swenson's, will fix it. Follow that sundae with a bottle of Come Back Sauce from Hal & Mal's on several baskets of crackers, and you can be happy for a while.

If you're feeling industrious, you can whip up some sacred Come Back Sauce in your own Cuisinart. You'll need the following ingredients: 3 cloves of garlic, 2 cups of mayonnaise, ¹/₂ cup of chili sauce, ¹/₂ cup of ketchup, 1 cup of salad oil, 2 tablespoons of black pepper, the juice of two lemons, 2 teaspoons of yellow mustard, 2 teaspoons of Worcestershire, 2 dashes of Tabasco sauce, and half an onion, grated. Dump it all in the Cuisi, and whirl away.

Come Back Sauce is an all-purpose dressing, good on everything as far as we can tell—salad, of course, and black-eyed peas and even pizza. A number of Jackson's local restaurants feature their own variations of Come Back, but Hal & Mal's version is the Queens' favorite. If you're a hopeless slackass, you can call Hal & Mal's at 1-601-948-0888, and they'll ship you out some for a modest fee.

DANGER PUDDING

For the uninitiated, Danger Pudding is made with a can of sweetened condensed milk. I don't know about you, but I can get happy just thinking about eating an entire can of Eagle Brand, just as it is, right out of the can. Malcolm White says when he was little, his mama used to give him a whole can of sweetened condensed milk to eat, all by himself, on his birthday; it was basically what he lived for every year.

To make Danger Pudding, you take your can, and without opening it, you boil it for an hour or so. Now, the people who make sweetened condensed milk are hip to this, and they say flat-out you shouldn't do this, ever. They feel so strongly about it, they actually print this warning right on the label: "Danger! Do not heat unopened can!" So be forewarned: You're risking your life and assorted kitchen parts by doing it. In my opinion, however, it's worth the hazard. All that sugar caramelizes, and it has about nine jillion fat grams, and this is why it's such strong medicine. You can actually make Danger Pudding with the fat-free sweetened condensed milk, and this will do if you're artery-conscious. But you shouldn't do any of this yourself because you could be killed. Come by my house, and I'll make it for us. I'm very brave.

MIMI'S BUTTERFINGER COOKIES

A surgeon general's report ranked Mississippi really high—in the fat demographics, that is. We finally get at the top of a national list, and look at what it is. The rest of the country is praying that we don't fall off and smash them. I personally have done my part to maintain our high standing in this regard. I generally eat like there's no tomorrow, or at least no lunch tomorrow. We can't just rest on our big fat laurels and hope to keep this high rating, however. We'll all have to participate. Here's a little something for anybody having trouble keeping those precious pounds on: Mimi's Butterfinger Cookies.

I wouldn't have thought it possible to improve on a Butterfinger candy bar, but danged if Tammy's mom, Mimi, didn't figure out a way. I think it's the combination of sweet and salty that makes this dish so completely irresistible. You need $1\frac{1}{2}$ cups of sugar, $1\frac{1}{3}$ cups of dark brown sugar, a stick of butter, 4 eggs (Mimi used just the whites, but when you read the rest of the ingredients, this seems laughable, like ordering everything on the menu but putting Equal in your tea—to save calories), and 3 running-over teaspoons of vanilla. Mix all that up. Then dump in $2\frac{1}{2}$ cups of chunky peanut butter, and stir that all up also. You need 2 cups of flour, a teaspoon of baking soda, and $\frac{1}{2}$ teaspoon of salt. Work those into the mix.

Now it's Butterfinger time. You can either use the BB's,

which are really easy to deal with, or you can get just regular Butterfinger candy bars—20 or so ounces' worth—cut 'em up, throw 'em in, and blend together the whole wondrous conglomeration. Drop teaspoon-sized blobs on a lightly greased cookie sheet, and bake them at 350 degrees for 7 to 9 minutes.

Funeral Food~
The Brighter Side of Death

When someone dies in the South, it's not altogether tragic. We always like to think that death has its advantages for the departed one—journey's end, sweet chariots, unbroken circles, and all that. For everyone left behind after the untimely passing, there's the unmistakable comfort of funeral food. When there's a death in a Southern town, everybody who has ever known anybody in the family has to take food to the home of the bereaved. It is practically a law. One of the Queens, Tammy, said there was a lady in her hometown who got up every morning of the world and fried a chicken first thing so that just in case somebody died that day, she could be on-the-spot with first-class funeral food.

Most of us are not quite that obsessive about fixing funeral food, but it's a tradition we have no plans to give up. Granted, it's a pain in the butt to have to stop whatever you're doing and make a casserole to give away, but we always remember that sooner or later some of our people will be departing, and all the funeral food will come home to roost with us. "The smaller the town, the better the food" is a pretty good rule for assessing funeral fare. In your bigger towns and cities, you might get the occasional ready-made cold-cut platter and once in a while a store-bought pie might slip in. But in a small town it's like a baking competition. Everybody who brings something will be checking out what everybody else brought—and talking about it, so one doesn't offer anything not homemade.

Even the most anguished, devoted family member can find some shred of consolation in funeral food. If there's a balm in Gilead, I'd be willing to bet it's made with cream of mushroom soup, Velveeta, or Cool Whip. Nearly all funeral food contains at least one of these staples. I don't care how fancy a gourmet cook you might think you are—you may not even allow Velveeta in your own personal kitchen—but I've yet to meet the palate too sophisticated for funeral food. In fact, I've observed that the snootier they are, the higher they pile those plates up. Everybody loves funeral food; it's a universal truth, and this is easy to explain. There's hardly anything quite as soothing as a warm casserole—especially a warm casserole that someone else made. That is, after all, one of the primary qualifications for good food: Someone else prepared it.

When one of my very favorite mamas, Hazel Rubenstein, mother to two of my favorite sons, Michael and Ted, died in

Booneville, way up in northeastern Mississippi, we were all transported to a celestial apex by the staggering quality and quantity of the funeral food. And let's face it, as I've earlier suggested, quantity is at least as important as quality. If it's the best morsel you ever put in your mouth but there's just a little dab of it, it will not satisfy as intended, but rather will serve as a major annoyance.

Well, at Hazel's last hurrah, not only did we have a delightfully embarrassing abundance of food at the house, there was funeral food at the funeral home as well. The funeral home had a big room with long tables in it, and all the friends of all the bereaved families could bring their food there for the solace of the mourners. This way you can mingle with everybody and not have to interrupt your grieving in order to have a snack. A fabulous innovation; I hope it spreads. As I recall, they also had a TV room, and this enabled the male mourners to grieve continually without missing a single major sporting event.

MISS LEXIE'S PINEAPPLE CASSEROLE

One of the very best things to come out of Hazel's funeral—and it's an ill wind, after all, that blows nobody good—was an extraordinary pineapple casserole brought by Hazel's friend Miss Lexie. This is truly one of nature's perfect foods, not just combining, as it does, sweet and salty, which would be enough of an accomplishment right there, but also having cheese in it.

What to Eat When Tragedy Strikes

Not many foods can satisfy the sweet, salty, and au gratin requirements at the same time. This is a very special dish. We stood around the table like vultures (albeit Queenly vultures) and ate it straight out of the casserole dish until it was gone. You couldn't risk putting some on your plate and going off somewhere to eat it before coming back for more. It was too good. We knew it would soon be gone, and so we just made sure that it went to its rightful diners, namely us. And since we were among family and our closest friends, we could get away with wolfing down an entire casserole ourselves and simply whisking the empty dish away out of sight before the other mourners arrived.

When you make this dish, I strongly urge you to double or, better, triple it; otherwise I can assure you there won't be enough. You want to drain a 20-ounce can of pineapple (in its own juice) chunks or tidbits. Save 3 tablespoons of the juice, and mix it with $1/2$ cup of sugar and 3 tablespoons of flour. Stir that mixture in with the pineapple and a cup of sharp grated cheese. (I've never tried making this with fat-free cheese and consider that blasphemous, but I have used some reduced-fat cheese when it was all I had, and it came out okay.) Dump all that into a greased casserole. Melt a stick of butter, and stir into it $1/2$ cup of Ritz Cracker crumbs; put all that on top of the pineapple mixture. Bake it at 350 degrees for 20 to 30 minutes, and prepare to be comforted.

Making the Best of a Bad Situation

Another occasion for substantial gatherings of people and mammoth feasts of fattening foods is the family reunion. There's very little on the surface to distinguish a family reunion feed from a funeral feed. There's an overabundance of food and family at both of them. At a family reunion, however, there's usually not a dead body, and there's virtually none of the relief from the icky family members, immediate and extended, that's provided by friends and comparative strangers at a funeral. All in all a funeral is much to be preferred over a family reunion, even if somebody *does* have to die for it. Most people I know would actually volunteer as designated dead guy at the funeral before they'd willingly attend a family reunion. Face it, at a family reunion there will hardly be a soul you can stand to be around for five minutes, and hordes of people you've dedicated your life to getting away from, all vying for your share of the coconut cake.

The only redeeming feature of a family reunion is the food itself. The Queens have come up with what we think is the best idea we ever heard in our entire lives. We're going to start having regular *familyless* reunions, complete with all our favorite foods, blankets on the ground, music, and games. And we're not going to invite a single soul from any of our families. We've entertained ourselves for several days just planning what-all food we'll absolutely have to have at the Familyless Reunion. Here's a fair summation of the A-list.

What to Eat When Tragedy Strikes

Fried chicken is mandatory, and it must be the skins-on variety. I can make excellent skinless fried chicken by marinating it in buttermilk for a few hours before flouring and frying it, but truly nothing on earth can compare to fried chicken skin. It's the very best part of the chicken, and we all know it. As a general rule, we're willing to give it up in day-to-day life, but this is, after all, a special occasion, and so we must insist on skin. BoPeep is truly the child of my heart and appetite. From the time that she had a tooth in her head, this little angel knew instinctively that the skin was the best part. I'd really hoped she'd have some inexplicable aversion to it; I pondered how much more chicken skin I could enjoy if my child didn't want hers. But this was not to be. If I were to leave a plate of fried chicken with skin sitting unattended for a nanosecond, I'd return to find a full platter of naked chicken. 'Peep would've picked all the skin off and sucked it down her greedy little gullet.

Deviled eggs—we can't have a Familyless Reunion without them. Someone else will definitely have to make them; they're a world-class pain to prepare. We've got to have the fried stuff—green tomatoes, okra, squash. It's all rolled in cornmeal before it's fried, so it's trouble, too, but so well worth it. One redeeming feature of cooking with okra is that when you cut the ends off the pods, you can stick them on your forehead and they will stay there all day, if you like. You can run down the street, and those okra tips will be sticking right there on your forehead. I once stuck them all over my face, including the tip of my nose, and wore them proudly while I cooked dinner for my guests. Of course, then everybody wanted some on their faces, too. I have a photo somewhere of this room full of people with okra stems on their foreheads—an intelligent bunch.

Foods that also made the A-list for the Familyless Reunion: chocolate pie, banana pudding, coconut cake, hot biscuits, corn on the cob, fresh lima beans, fresh lady peas, that awful green bean casserole with the onion rings on top that somebody always brings and we always eat it even though it's lethal, ribs, cornbread, Louisiana strawberries and homemade shortcake, blackberry cobbler, potato salad, sliced-right-off-the-vine tomatoes, homemade mayonnaise, and oceans of sweet iced tea.

What to Eat Before and After an Assignation

Well, "before" is a no-brainer; you can't eat a damn thing. If you do, your stomach will pooch out like you're twelve months pregnant, and it will ruin the lines of your trashy lingerie. And this is truly tragic. I don't think there's been any lingerie ever designed that will camouflage an engorged belly. A smock is all I can think of that would successfully conceal that you have eaten Chicago. Damn hard to look sexy in a smock. (If you've ever actually been pregnant, you can attest to this.)

What to Eat When Tragedy Strikes

You can get flat on your back as soon as possible—that helps. Your stomach always looks better if you're flat on your back. Of course, if it's so early in a relationship that reclining hasn't been considered, then this might appear unseemly. Location can also be a problem. I've found there are hardly any good places to lie down at the movies. Some bars are wisely addressing this situation and providing full-length sofas for overstuffed patrons. Encourage such attention to customer service by frequenting these establishments often.

Of course, as long as you're fully clothed, you can hide a lot—even if you just sit with your purse in your lap. If your companion becomes unexpectedly amorous soon after a large meal, stall him. Delay any activity that would necessitate the removal of any of your clothing until digestion has been completed. If you know in advance that this is to be his lucky night, then by all means postpone dinner.

After the fact anything is the limit. You can eat as much as you want of whatever you want. Even if he's still around, post-frolic, you can put on a big garment and look cute while you clean out the refrigerator with your own face. The very best eating, however, is to be enjoyed solo. Send him home, lock all the doors, pile up in the bed with a black-and-white movie, and have yourself a private smorgasbord. Two syllables: Hea-ven.

13

Queenly Entertainment

ROAD TRIPS AND THE
WFW LUNCHEON CLUB

The Queens are always searching for new entertainment, and so it was inevitable that sooner or later we'd venture to one of Mississippi's many casinos. Last time I checked, I think we had more casinos than gas stations or, as the indigenous folk would say, "fillin' stations." So far, in our esteemed opinion, the only one worth going to is the Silver Star in Philadelphia, Mississippi, on the Choctaw Indian reservation, and it's pretty fine. They have a world-class spa and a fabulous golf course that people, golfing types, fly in from everywhere to play. The very notion of all this is hilarious and ironic to anyone who has ever been to Philadelphia, Mississippi, pre-casino. You can drive through Neshoba County for miles, and you'll see nothing but red dirt, red dirt, red dirt—BIG CASINO—red dirt, red dirt, red dirt. Smack dab in the very epicenter of nowhere is the stunning hotel with golf course, spa, and casino.

But unfortunately we were late in discovering the Silver Star, and our first journey into the cosmos of Mississippi gambling was a jarring experience. There aren't any casinos in Jackson, where we live, because of some twisty-windy law that says that we can have gambling only if it's on a boat floating in a moving body of water or on an Indian reservation. At any rate I complained one evening that I was probably the only person on the planet who had not been to one of our state's casinos, and so one of the Queens, Tammy, and I struck out for Vicksburg. Tammy had previously been to casinos on the Gulf Coast, but she'd never tried Vicksburg's. I don't know what her expectations were for the evening. The only casinos I myself had ever been in were onboard big cruise ships, so my hopes were high. I expected that everyone would be beautifully dressed and well mannered, sun-kissed and sophisticated. It certainly never occurred to me to question whether our fellow patrons would have teeth.

I now realize that I have always taken teeth for granted in my everyday life. Most everyone I encounter in my appointed rounds has a full set of them. So accustomed have I become to people having teeth, and plenty of them, it comes as a shock to me whenever I find myself in the presence of an individual over the age of eight who is without them. I am taken aback somewhat by the sight of a snaggletoothed adult.

The crowds parted wherever we walked, as if we were visiting royalty or movie stars. There must have been a large, perhaps national, convention in town, of men with no chins and women with fat arms. Our dress also set us apart from the misbegotten throng. As I recall, we had on skirts and blouses and stockings and shoes—things like that. You know, no ball gowns or anything, but like you would dress for some special event—such as being seen in public. We didn't wear skintight jeans wedged fetchingly up our butts or T-shirts with legends like "A Little Poontang Never Hurt Anybody." We didn't rat our hair up anywhere near enough for this crowd, and our makeup was on the tasteful side. We weren't even once tempted to spit on the floor. Our conversation was subdued, audible only to each other, and it was not punctuated by boisterous high-fives.

We did see three men of the type that I personally judge "normal." They were dressed in slacks and sports shirts, with room to breathe in both. They looked as peculiar there as Tammy and I did. The other 35,000 males there that evening were dressed in one of two prevailing shirt styles: (1) the nasty tank top, cut low enough on all sides to reveal an overabundance of body (especially back) hair, and stretched over the mandatory beer gut so tightly, they looked like huge hairy sacks of flour, and (2) the cowboy-stud shirt, a western shirt that belonged to one's little brother—so small that only the bottom two snaps can be fastened, and the hairy beer gut protrudes from the gaps. We likewise took note of the waitresses' outfits. It's been at least two decades since I've seen women dressed in such mortifying attire in the workplace. These waitresses have brought back the short-skirt-with-petticoats-so-you-can-see-their-ruffled-panties look, with the low-cut bodices that thrust their breasts out into the middle of the room.

We went to the buffet and thoroughly enjoyed it, I must say. Like all true Southerners, we consider fat a delicacy. We weren't disappointed. I can safely say I've never had a better meal at any pancake house in the country, and it was all-you-can-eat to boot. We didn't gamble. Not one thin dime. We were much too intimidated by the sweaty masses. We didn't try another Vicksburg casino since my friend Fran had recommended this one as having the best people. All I can say is, if those are the "best" ones, I can't imagine the lesser ones. If I can't have James Bond in Monte Carlo in a white dinner jacket, I'd just as soon be playing bingo at the church.

Out of Pocket

The Queens do love a road trip. Even if it's just for the day, our favorite thing is to be Out of Pocket. As soon as we get in a vehicle of any kind, headed anywhere, as long as the adventure pertains in any way to foolishness, we're Out of Pocket. As the doors shut behind each new addition to the passenger list, we exchange wicked looks and declare in chorus, "We're officially Out of Pocket!" And off we go.

Our most memorable trip ever was a trip to Graceland. One of the Queens, Tammy, had a guy friend who was coming to visit her, and for some reason he needed to be picked up in Memphis. So what we did, as if it made perfect sense, was to rent a big old tour bus. A real one, like the ones rock stars use on the road. We rented it for the day and went to Memphis in it. Two of the Tammys on the trip were in the Junior League. (I wouldn't have believed it myself; but they did emerge from the experience unscathed.) As it happened, the very day that we had chosen was also the day of some important event at the Junior League house, and as past presidents, they were expected to attend. One Tammy had declined weeks before, but the other Tammy had neglected to do so, and so she called the Junior League headquarters from the bus. Now, we had Delbert McClinton wailing on the stereo, the Tammys were all bouncing around dancing and squealing in that endearing girl-ish fashion for which we are famous, the bus itself was making a fair amount of noise, and Tammy, she just called them up and in a perfectly calm tone said, "I am so sorry I won't be able to be there today after all. A number of things have come up, and I'm out of pocket." At which we all fell on the floor, whooping and gasping for breath. And this was the genesis of

"Out of Pocket" to designate both our destination and our mode of travel.

We were on our way to Memphis on the bus. Tammy had told her friend just to go to Graceland and wait for his ride. "You'll be picked up" is all she had said. All the way to Memphis, we tried on trashy lingerie. Everybody brought every article of pretty dritties she owned, and we tried them all on in every possible combination, selecting just the right thing to wear to Graceland. Even though Elvis would not actually be there, we wanted to dress appropriately. We decided that Tammy's high heels weren't high enough, and so when we got to Memphis a little early, we went in search of spikes for her. We happened to be in a neighborhood of Memphis that was filled with pawnshops. The sight of all those pawnshops got Tammy to thinking about handcuffs—the Queens love handcuffs—and soon everybody was clamoring for handcuffs. We stopped at a number of pawnshops and went in, wearing our carefully selected outfits under our fur coats. Nobody had handcuffs. All they had was some of the very biggest gold chains we'd ever seen. I don't think those chains exist anywhere outside of pawnshops—pawnshops in Memphis, for that matter. None of us has ever seen their likes anywhere before or since. Handcuffless, we continued the search for trashy shoes for Tammy. You just can't wear a sensible midheel with a black lace teddy. It contradicts the whole look. We finally found what we wanted. Then on to Graceland.

As we pulled into the parking lot of the souvenir mall across the street from Graceland, we sighted Tammy's guy, standing on the corner with his suitcase, watching the cars whiz by. He never so much as glanced at our bus, so totally unsuspecting was he that it was ours. We rumbled into the parking lot and debarked. As we strode across the parking lot with our high heels clicking on the pavement, we shrugged off our fur coats—despite the frosty wind—to reveal our outfits: black heels, black tights, and black lace teddies. We looked like we had escaped from a Robert Palmer "Addicted to Love" recording session. Tammy's fellow followed the gaze of the quickly accumulating crowd in the parking lot, and his little face just lit right up when he saw us. He seemed genuinely glad to see us. I guess the reasons were obvious: partly because he was freezing and sick of standing on the corner waiting for a ride, and partly because here was a whole big gang of women from Mississippi in black lace underwear walking across the parking lot with half of Memphis slamming on brakes to gawk at them—and they were there to meet him. I believe he walked a little taller that day.

Searching for the Wildest F——— in the World

One of the Queens, Tammy, I believe it was, worked for a number of years with a very quiet little woman named Sandy.

Now, our Tammy was always quite forthcoming with all the details of her dating life, but Sandy never said a word about her own. To the contrary, Sandy never admitted to even having dates. If Sandy had been named Goody, her last name would have been FourShoes—she was plainly that pure. Well, she was quiet anyway. So time passed, and Sandy moved away. But by and by, as circumstance would have it, a bunch of us happened to be having cocktails one evening in Jackson with a guy-friend of ours who's a well-known blabbermouth. This is one of his more endearing qualities. In the course of the conversations, which naturally included extensive discussion on the behavior of others, Sandy's name came up. Someone brought her name up as an example of a really boring person to go out with, should anyone be in the market for such. With this, the blabbermouth almost spewed beer out his nose, so anxious was he to blab what-all he knew. He said something like *"au contraire"*—he may have even used those exact words—he's that type.

At any rate he indicated that we clearly did not know jack-shit about our friend Sandy. He said that he talked to this guy, Jack, who told him he had taken Sandy out for three whole months and never got the time of day from her. At this point we're all going, Yeah, that's the Sandy we know. "But *then*," he said, his tone dripping with portents of things to come. We were breathless, waiting. He toyed with us for as long as he thought it safe, and then he went on. Jack had reported to him that after the three months of dating, he somehow "cornered her one night." Now, we were real curious as to what that meant. Anyway, he cornered her one night, and in Jack's words, "She was the wildest f—— in the *world!*"

And that was all the blabbermouth said. He then just sat there, looking pleased with himself, like he had just performed something significant for the universe, and we just sat there looking back at him, waiting, obviously, for the rest of the story. He kept on sitting there, grinning. Finally, we demanded him to tell us the rest of it. He confessed that was all he knew. Jack said she was the wildest f—— in the world, and that was that. We were incredulous. "That's it?" we protested. "A guy tells you that some woman, whom you happen to know, is the wildest f—— in the world and then clams up, and you let him get away with it?" Surely he didn't expected us to believe that he hadn't immediately demanded to know details. Apparently that was precisely what he wanted us to believe. He swore up and down that when he heard the words, he was so completely blown away that he was at a loss for words; then Jack left.

So now here we all were—ravaged with curiosity about what specifically it was that Sandy did that prompted Jack, who was quite the hound, to rank her as the number-one wildest in the world. We were beating the blabbermouth about the head and shoulders with our purses and proclaiming him to be the most worthless piece of crap we had ever encountered in this life and insisted that he get up and go call Jack right then and get all the info we needed. "Jack doesn't live here anymore" was all we got for our trouble, and the blabbermouth got big welts all over from us whacking on him. No more than he deserved.

And so the Queens had a new mission in life: to be the Wildest F—— in the World (the WFW). But first we needed some outside assistance. We decided to hold focus groups— get a few luncheon speakers, as it were. We would call up a guy we knew who we thought had some sense, and we'd ask him to meet us for lunch. He, of course, would eagerly accept. When he arrived, he would find himself the only man at the table. This would initially please him, I think, and then we would notice just a trace of uneasiness creeping in. Good. (We read an Italian proverb once that said, and we believe it is true, "The fear of women is the basis of good health." We like that.) We'd sit close up to him and smile and pat a lot, and he'd start getting squirmy. Then we'd tell him, "You are our luncheon speaker." After his blank look we would explain that we wanted him to speak to our little group of Queens about something of keen interest to us, and he'd ask what was that, and we'd reveal his topic. "We want you to talk—in great detail—about what, in your considered opinion, we—hypothetically speaking—would have to do in order to qualify as the Wildest F—— in the World."

His eyes would be rolling back in his head; I swear, delirium just comes on quick, doesn't it? We'd persist, "Is it clothes? Trashy lingerie? Props? Games? Talking dirty? Does it involve food?" He'd look wordlessly from face to face and make some muffled Porky Pig sounds, but we would not relent. Sooner or later, we'd wear him down and he'd give us some little shred of usable information.

The best tip we got was from our best buddy, Bob, who is this big blond bear of a guy who is more fun than just about anybody. What Bob told us was this: "You worry too much about how you look, what you wear, and it has nothing to do with any of that." He said that it didn't even matter that our bodies weren't perfect, although he was quick to say he was quite certain that our own personal bodies *were* perfect. He said all that mattered—*all* that mattered—was enthusiasm. Enthusiasm! Well, in that case, we should be shoo-ins. We're nothing if not enthusiastic. We pressed him further. We wanted to be absolutely certain that if there was something to be done, we were doing it. He insisted that unbridled enthusiasm was our ticket to stardom. We took him at his word, and that was the last meeting of the WFW Luncheon Club.

14

So You Declare Yourself a Queen

NOW WHAT?

Well, let me just tell you what life has been like for me since I became a Sweet Potato Queen. Some days I do not do jackshit. Now, before you scoff, let me tell you that not doing jackshit is not the simple act of sloth that it may appear to the uninitiated. On the contrary, not doing jackshit is, for some blighted individuals, next to impossible. They seem compelled, as if by some invisible force, to engage themselves in constant busy-ness. On vacations they must see everything in Europe in eight days.

At home they're always running endless errands. At work they are always *working*. There's no end to it, and I do not, for the life of me, see how they can bear their lives.

Some years ago my sister, Judy, and I discovered our innate ability to not do jackshit. It was during our fifth trip to Cozumel that particular year that we noticed a pattern. Some guy in the airport in New Orleans struck up a conversation with us and was very curious as to why we would be going to Cozumel, or anywhere else, five times in one year.

"Do you snorkel?"

"No."

"Sightsee?"

"Certainly not."

"Parasail?"

"Do we look like we parasail?" (We're large women.)

"Do you dive?"

"No, but we like the look of all the macho housewives who hang around town in their diving shoes and wet suits with knives strapped to their legs, and we're considering getting our own leg-knives."

He pressed on: "Well, what *do* you do?"

In unison we responded, "We don't do jackshit! As a matter of fact," we said, "we're gonna start not doing jackshit as soon as we get on this plane, and furthermore, we can probably teach you to not do jackshit, too, and it will immeasurably enhance the remainder of your life."

So You Declare Yourself a Queen

And so we did, and he left us a much happier man for the whole thing.

Here's what a typical day of not doing jackshit back at home looks like: I rise early to greet the dawn, smell the honeysuckle as the sun first warms it, hear the mockingbird's earliest song, and begin not doing jackshit. I cause massive breakfasts to be prepared and shared. Calais—rice cakes like deep-fried bread pudding with pecans—blueberry muffins with lemon curd, cheese grits, regular grits with New Orleans grillades, waffles, and, of course, bacon—lots and lots of bacon. I think there's an unwritten law that should be written: You can never have too much bacon. And fresh-squoze orange juice by the bucket. (You say *squeezed* if you want to, my orange juice will be *squoze*.)

After breakfast it's necessary to lounge for a bit, waiting for the sun to get hot enough to bask myself. And I bask away—to Hell with the naysayers. Then it's time for cool, refreshing—possibly rum—drinks. Lying alternately in the sun and shade, I read novels that contain lots of descriptions of clothing and food. (Don't you just love to know what everybody was wearing and what-all they had to eat? I know I do.) Sometime along in here a light lunch will appear.

The gentlest of breezes blows across my terrace, making a nap in the shade irresistible. Then I drift awake to watch the trained yellow butterflies flitting about the backyard. When my sister, Judy, seeks a small diversion from not doing jackshit, she trains butterflies. Her tribulations with her first husband, the unsavory Ole Shep, sort of tired her out for dealing with people and dogs. So she trained a covey of yellow butterflies for my backyard. You've got to hand it to butterflies—they're damn quiet.

Sometimes, late in the afternoon, when the air would be unbearably heavy were it not for the breeze, there's music. A gospel choir might sing softly—or real loud, depending on my mood. Or maybe Etta James will drop by. Or Van Morrison. Or Aaron Neville. If I'm feeling sporty, Eric Clapton and Delbert McClinton might happen in, and if they do, they'll not be allowed to leave. Friends may come over to shoot dart guns at a beauty pageant on TV, and we'll eat Chocolate Stuff and fried chicken drummettes and drink margaritas.

Much later I take a big bath. Baths are real slo-o-o-ow around here. There's just no telling how long I might soak in that tub, but sooner or later I amble on off to bed, where I lie in the dark, listening to the sound of the breeze in the live oaks, high on the scent of the gardenias blooming outside my window, and wait for the moon to rise. Now, if you got a better idea of how to spend your days, I'd sure like to hear about it.

"Do what you will wish you had done when you are old." Everybody's heard this sage advice. Since I first heard it when I was still quite young myself, there aren't just a whole lot of things that I flat-out *haven't* done. Pretty much everything that came up required a choice, and I knew right off the bat, with very little pondering, what I would wish I had done. I'd wish I had done it all, and therefore I did it.

It goes beyond just the doing or not doing, though. If you decide in favor of doing and it turns out to be good, do a lot of it. You never know how short the supply might be. Some things in life are just so sweet—and sweet is really not strong enough—I mean, so soothing and delicious that sometimes the memory of them is all you need to get by. You can just close your eyes and put yourself there in an instant. Your mouth waters, your eyes tear up, your heart beats fast, and it's hard to catch your breath.

Kissing Bill French was one of those sweet things in my life. Bill French—and we always called him by both names, never just Bill—was, in my considered opinion, the Best Kisser in the History of the Entire World, living or dead. He just had a magic mouth. I could die happy right this minute if I could die kissing Bill French. We were never even boyfriend and girl-friend or anything like that, just good buddies. But somehow, for some reason, he kissed me one night. I knew he was *fixing* to; you can always tell, you know. I had my spiel all ready about us being just friends and all. But I let him kiss me that one time. And it just about melted the fillings in my teeth. I was like a dog eating peanut butter; I just couldn't qui-I-I-ite get through kissing him.

Anyway, kissing Bill French was one of those incredibly

sweet things that, when times are really bad, I could just think about and feel better. I'd say to myself, "You know, if I wanted to, I could just get in my car and drive to Birmingham and kiss Bill French and feel a whole lot better." No matter that it wasn't actually feasible, that both of us were married to somebody else, that we'd had no contact in years, that I wouldn't even really know how to find him. It was just something I held out to myself. And I always felt like sometime maybe, sooner or later, our paths would cross again, and I could get me one or two of his kisses and no harm done.

And then one day on an impulse I called a mutual friend, Peter Binder, in Birmingham, and we were yakking away about old times and I mentioned Bill French. Peter was suddenly silent. Well, come to find out, Bill French had been killed in a plane crash a year or so before, and nobody knew how to call me. It hit me like an avalanche. I grieved and grieved over it. To find out that not only was he gone, he had *been* gone—just undid me. I will never again in this life kiss Bill French, and it makes it a little bit harder to go on.

And then they told me that Charlie Jacobs was dead. Charlie was a musician in a band called the Tangents that was popular all over the South in the 1980s. I couldn't go to the funeral. Call me a wuss. I swear I did it out of kindness to everybody else who would be there. I knew I'd be rolling around wailing if I went, so I didn't go. I did, however, find an old tape I had of the Tangents playing live at the George Street

So You Declare Yourself a Queen

Grocery, a great old pub in Jackson. I put that tape on, and Charlie was singing "Love and Pain." I lay down on the floor between the speakers and closed my eyes. I was *there*. I could see him. Watching Charlie Jacobs perform was as good as hearing him, which is saying a lot. He didn't *play* the music; he *was* the music. The harp and the sax and that raspy, sexy voice of his—that's just how the music got *out* of him. His body contorted, face twisting, grimacing, grinning, eyes rolled up, fluttering, or squeezed shut tight, oceans of sweat streaming down his body, shining in the spotlight. And the music just carrying him—and me—away. I'd dance to every note he played, sweating every bit as much. I could not resist it.

I can listen to that tape, and as much as my heart sings with the sweetness of the memories, the knowledge that he's gone makes me feel like my whole body has turned to liquid and it's coming out my eyes—melting, melting. When it's over, I'll just be a pile of old clothes on the floor, like the Wicked Witch in Oz.

Here's the deal, though: One day, one day I'll get to Heaven, and when I do, the first thing I'm going to do is drink a cold one with my daddy and pet my old dog Randy, and then I'll get Charlie to play and sing, and I'm gonna dance till I drop. And in between sets, and on all the slow songs, I'm gonna kiss Bill French. Then I'll know for *sure* I'm in Heaven.

Some guy-type buddies of my youth lived for a time in a veritable garden spot that they lovingly, if misguidedly, referred to as The Ranch. If you've ever been to the South and taken a drive down a country road, you'd have spied out in the middle of a field an old abandoned shack. If you were somewhere in the western part of Hinds County, Mississippi, you may have seen the actual ranch. It was an absolute hovel. I have no idea if they even paid rent; there's an excellent chance they were merely squatting. However, back in the mid-1970s, it suited them just fine. They held huge wild parties, thinking themselves to be invisible out there in Podunk, as it were. I guess they didn't believe anybody would think it curious that there were a couple hundred cars parked around this shack in the middle of nowhere.

Anyway, a stranger came to their door one day. He was singularly unattractive—very little hair covering his hideous, sore-wracked skin, just generally ratty and nasty looking. But as is often said of the unbeautiful of the world, he had a great personality. He came to be known as "Funkdog," because he was, in fact, a dog, and he was really funky. He came around regularly, and the boys would feed him and talk to him, but no one could quite bring themselves to actually touch him. And so they started this thing of petting Funkdog with a small stick. He would come and sit at a respectful distance, I guess knowing himself to be unclean, and eagerly await being petted and scratched with his stick. That image always just made me want to bawl, and now I think I know why.

So You Declare Yourself a Queen

I think Funkdog being petted with his stick is a perfect metaphor for what can happen to any of us in this life if we don't pay attention. In any area of our lives, things can go from great, to not so hot, to downright unspeakable, and do it so gradually that we keep downshifting our expectations to correspond with our current situation. We settle for less and less and tell ourselves "It's not so bad" until finally one day we wake up and we are, in effect, hairless and scabby, just hoping to get petted with a stick for a little while. You can forget what it used to feel like to feel good about life; feeling rotten—or just a low-grade funk—seems normal and therefore acceptable. I just don't believe that God intended for any of his creatures to be petted with sticks. If some area of your life sucks—do something else. Life is too short—and too long—to spend it being miserable. Life may indeed be short, but it is, for a fact, wide. It is high time we started settling for more.

The truth is that real life sometimes doesn't turn out to be exactly what we'd planned or dreamed. This disparity occurs with alarming frequency. But hey, you've got to do whatever's necessary to live, to take care of yourself and your kids. There are some pretty awful jobs out there, and real people are having to do them every day. My friend Scott told me about meeting a lovely young woman who worked, I swear to you, as a full-time chicken plucker. The girl stands by a conveyor belt and pulls the feathers off chickens all day long. He said to her, with intense emotion, "I can't imagine that. You must have *the* most boring job in the whole world." And do you know, she lit up like a lightning bug and responded seriously, "Oh, no. You get a brand-new chicken every thirty seconds!"

She has what is undoubtedly the most overdeveloped sense of optimism—or she is the most joyfully creative soul there ever was. If a chicken plucker is truly fulfilled in her work, I certainly applaud that. If, however, she has merely settled for less and is dissatisfied—if anyone is spending life toiling away at work you despise—I'd have to say authoritatively that God doesn't make chicken pluckers; people make chicken pluckers, and if you don't want to be one, then by God, don't.

But maybe your job isn't all that terrible. Your marriage is not really hideous; it's just sort of *beige*. Flat, dull, lifeless— these are not good adjectives when they refer to your hair; they are infinitely worse if they apply to your life. If you are stuck, sweating, on a sandbar in the river of your life, you've got to find a way back into those swift, effervescent currents of joy that are your birthright.

If you need to feel sexy, buy yourself a pair of high-heeled shoes or some trashy lingerie. If you need to laugh, I recommend that you order yourself a pair of fake teeth, as I did, called Dr. Bukk's Teef. They fit over your own teeth like a mouthpiece used in contact sports. They look utterly real, and they're the worst-looking things you ever saw in your life, unless you go to the Waffle House a lot. There are many styles to choose from, and I have two of them: Summer Teef—some 'r' here, some 'r' not—and Sole Survivor, featuring a single snaggly-looking tooth somewhat off center, bearing a gold crown with a heart carved in it. I just love the way that flash of gold catches the light. You can't fully imagine, without having seen them, the dramatic effect these teef have on one's appearance. And on one's disposition. I'm wearing mine right this minute, and every once in a while, I glance in the mirror and grin. Perks me up no end.

(If you want some, and I know you do, you can call Dr. Bukk right up on her toll-free number, which is 1-800-925-BUKK [2855], and you can have your teef by the very next day. When you receive them, you're officially a member of the Bukk Fambly, and as such you'll need a new name to go with your new identity. Choose one and send it in, and you'll receive the Bukk Fambly newsletter on a somewhat irregular basis. My Bukk Fambly name is "Gemi Moore." And when you order your teef, you be sure and tell them I sent you.)

You can wear your Bukk teef and your high heels and trashy lingerie to the grocery store if you want to, or you can just prance around in them at home and enjoy being a goose all by yourself. Or you can just not do jackshit. Sometimes that's enough. You don't have to move or change jobs or leave your husband or unnaturally alter your state of consciousness. We're not after an altered state; we're after our True State—

unbridled joy. The adventurer Norman Vaughan, who's completed a dozen or so of those punishing dogsled races called Iditarods and, in his nineties, is still doing them, said, "The only death you die is the one you die every day by not living." And George Eliot wrote, "It is never too late to be what you might have been."

We thought all that is some mighty fine advice, and we turned out to be Sweet Potato Queens. It's working for us. I think you should give it a try.

Not ready to part with the Queens yet? Y'all come see us at our Web site,

www.sweetpotatoqueens.com

and bring your mommer 'n 'em.

Acknowledgments

There are a great many people to whom I'm deeply and proudly indebted. If I start naming at Crown Publishing, the list will be longer than the book—these folks have been so good to me. Of course, I'm fully aware that they all want to be Queens or to receive the Promise, but they've been nice nonetheless, and I appreciate it. Teresa Nicholas, Sue Carswell, and Rachel Kahan have exhibited extraordinary enthusiasm for the Sweet Potato Queens and this book from the very beginning, and I feel confident in promising them a fair shot at being Wannabes in the foreseeable future as a reward for their hard work and steadfast loyalty. Steve Wallace and Brian

Belfiglio are definitely in the running for Consort. Everyone at Crown has a standing invitation to the parade, and on behalf of all the Queens, I promise you'll have a Big Time.

JoAnne Prichard, my editor, and her husband, Willie Morris, have gone so far out of their way to help me, it wears me out even to think about what-all I'll likely have to do to pay them back. Suffice it to say it will involve unseemly amounts of biscuits and fried chicken (with skin).

Malcolm White—what can I say? If there had been no Mal's St. Paddy's Day parade or *Diddy Wah Diddy*, I guess I'd have just joined the Junior League, and then where would we be?

Johnny Evans at Lemuria Bookstore and Roy Blount, Jr., have been so encouraging to me, I guess they'll have to go on the list for biscuits and chicken, too.

Not everyone has the good fortune that I had of being born into a whole family of funny people. My sister, Judy, is funnier than I am. My mother, bless her, has never had a boring day. The leader of the bunch was, of course, my daddy, who taught us the invaluable lesson of Simultaneous Reverence and Irreverence. Either without the other can be deadly.

All the Sweet Potato Queens, past and present, have my undying love and loyalty. As you read this list, please imagine the strains of the "Twentieth Century–Fox Fanfare"—it's only fitting:

ACKNOWLEDGMENTS

Mona Britt Shumake

Cheri Anglin

Vivian Pigott White

Cynthia Hewes Speetjens

Lyla Gibson Elliot

Marsha McInturff

Carol Puckett Daily

Annie Laurie McRee

Annelle Primos Barnett

Elizabeth (Pippa) Perry Jackson

Donna Kennedy Sones

Sylvia Stewart

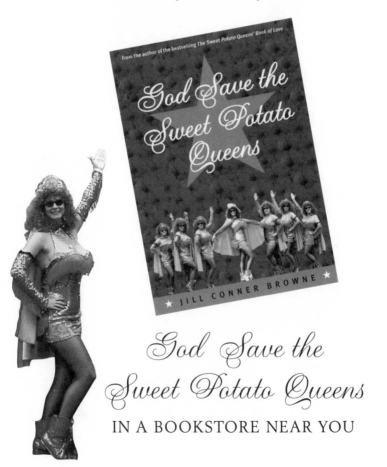

No, It's a Hole in the Head We Don't Need

Apparently a few readers—all men, if memory serves—somehow deduced from *SPQBOL* that we do not need them. One of them, in fact, recently asked me to compile a list of the top five or ten reasons Sweet Potato Queens don't need men. I thought and I thought about that. I must confess, I failed utterly in this task. After all, I asked myself, if there were no men, Aretha would have had no cause to sing "R-E-S-P-E-C-T," without which the world would be severely deprived. Bonnie Raitt would never have sung, "I wanna man to love me like my backbone was his own," and then where would we be? I could go on and on, but also consider this: If not men, then who would ever sing to us such memorable words as "I wanna drink your bathwater, baby"? Only a man would ever even think of such a thing. If there were no men, there would be no Johnnie Taylor to sing about the "Big Head Hundreds" and what all he wants to buy us with them. Oh, yes, sisters, we need men all right. We need them and we love them for these and many other reasons. The one and only reason I could think of that would justify our saying that we don't need men is this: We cannot borrow their shoes.

Okay, so we've gone and admitted that we need men. The problem then becomes, as related to us by many of our sisters: Where do you find them? This has just never been a problem for the Queens, as you may well imagine. Our problem is usually more along the lines of keeping the numbers manageable; therefore, we are in an excellent position to offer advice—which we would, of course, do whether we have any knowledge or experience in the matter at all and so, as it turns out in this particular case we do have some of both, though.

"They makin' 'em thangs ever'day," my daddy, who was very wise indeed, always said. Now, granted, he was referring to some manufactured product, but we can certainly give it just the slightest stretch, and it easily applies to men as well, at least in our minds, where, as you know, anything can happen and often does. The fact that they makin' 'em thangs ever'day just shows us, to our great relief, that there is no shortage. Men are in plentiful and readily available supply at all times. This is a big load off our minds, because they are so dang much trouble once you have them, that if you had to go out and hunt and scrounge around for them to begin with, well, it just might not even be cost-effective.

So, if men are everywhere, just waiting for us to pluck them off the vine, then the next question is: Which vine? Indeed, it is our experience that there are so many of them, at every turn, it is easy to get overwhelmed or even jaded and just not even bother plucking any of them. This is not a good set of circumstances. It feels awful, and we find, upon further examination, that it is often an early symptom of a hormonal imbalance; so whenever one of the Queens expresses a dis-interest in men, we all immediately gang up on her and make her assess her hormones. If it's not her hormones, it may just be that she's bored with the current crop and needs a change, just like your cat will be completely enthralled with that fake bird on a bungee cord with the bells and feathers and strings hanging off of it, will play with it for hours on end and then, suddenly, it's over. The thrill, as our beloved B. B. King says so well, is gone.

When this happens, there's nothing for it but another trip to PetSmart to get a new cat toy. Sometimes you just got to have a new cat toy. But you know how it is, you go to PetSmart and there's aisle after aisle of nothing but cat toys as far as the eye can see, and they all look pretty good. I mean, it's the same basic premise with all of them—they're on some kind of springy cord attached to a stick, they all have things that jiggle and wiggle and catch your eye. Some are bigger than others, some make more noise, some are fancier while others are more no-frills and serviceable. But you can't really try them out in the store. Oh, I know, they encourage you to bring your pets in there and all that, and that may work fine with some dogs, but cats are just not really who you want to take to the mall, now are they? Even that most famous of Southern cats, Willie Morris's own Spit McGee, is not a good shopper. Cats just don't get the theory of going to the store to look at new stuff. And anyway, most of the cat toys are sealed up in wrappers, so you couldn't try them out in the store even if you could induce your cat to go shopping with you. And would you really want to buy a floor-demo cat toy for your kitty? So it is with us, sisters.

There's tons of men out there, but the only way to know if you like them is to try them out for a while. Mercy, how do you settle on one or two to try? A number of folks have shared their Rules for Dating with us. From Pensacola, Susi writes that when she and her friends were in their thirties they had the ten-year rule—you couldn't date anybody more than ten years younger or older than yourself. But Marjorie, from another Southern state, writes that, at sixty-five, she is beginning to find her fifty-year-old lover a bit old for her! Yippee! is just all I can say to that. Now that they are older and, we believe, wiser, they have amended this to the new

Mommer'n'em Rule, which requires that you must be younger than his mama and have never dated his daddy. The Menopause Mafia of Louisiana (they are all named "Taffy" because they're all teachers—and teachers get chewed on many times each day) has as its number one rule: Never date a man whose mama is not dead.

Well, the Queens have come up with a system that works for us. We find we do best in situations when we can really focus our energies and attention. For this we need a theme, and that is what we are recommending to you today: Theme Dating. It doesn't really narrow the field, just your area of focus for the moment, but for that reason makes the field more manageable for you. The theme is completely arbitrary and at your total discretion. You may select any theme, pursue it for as long as it amuses you, and then change it, with no prior warning to anyone else. It's your theme, do with it what you will. As I said, a bunch of the Queens are married and so their themes are pretty much set, for the time being anyway. For the rest of us, the theme is a constant source of entertainment. We had a long-running Jewish theme there for a while. We dated only Jewish men. At the outset, I recalled a conversation that had taken place many years before with my good friend Helen Murphey Austin, whom I actually credit with introducing me to the Joys of Jews. She was dating a man named Edward Cohen—a Jew who has grown up to be a very fine screenwriter and recent author of *The Peddler's Grandson,* which is the story of his growing up Jewish in the South. Helen and Edward got me to go out with Edward's best friend, who just so happened to be Jewish as well, named Ralph Salomon. To provide the extremely little persuasion it took to get me to go out with Ralph, truly one of the most handsome men I have ever dated, Helen assured me that "Jewish men and Southern [non-Jewish] women get along like a house afire." That may sound like, may indeed be, a cliché, but it is nonetheless true. You have only to consider the average house and then visualize it completely engulfed in flames to know you've got a fair amount of energy and excitement going on. A blazing house can be loud, but it is certainly not boring, and I can guarantee you will never forget your house burning up— or down, as you prefer. And of course, one thing you can always count on with a fire of any kind—it's damn hot, and with one of this magnitude, even when it dies down, it'll still keep you warm for a long, long time. Oh, my, yes, we do love Jewish men.

For the last good while, though, we have been on a Bob theme. This is not as limiting as you might think on first examination. Just to show you how very versatile this theme theory is: You've got your Roberts, your Robs, your Berts, your Bobbys, Robbys, Berties, in addition to your basic Bobs. And half the men on the planet are named Robert, or at least their middle name is Robert. Then there's the surname factor— Roberts, Robertsons, and the like. We are just covered up in

No, It's a Hole in the Head We Don't Need

Bobs and/or Bob derivatives. Then there's the battery-oper-
ated boyfriend (BOB) that never lets us down. Yeah, buddy, as
long as them Eveready boys stay in bidness, we can rest easy.
BOBs, gotta love 'em.

I was in Santa Monica not long ago with one of the
Queens, Tammy, and we met a very fine young man at the
Starting Line athletic shoe store. (If you are ever in Santa
Monica, go there and buy your sports shoes—it is the only
place I have ever been where they (a) actually give a rat's ass
if your shoes fit; (b) actually know how to determine whether
or not they do; and amazingly (c) won't sell you a pair of shoes
that do not fit perfectly.) So me and Tammy are in the Starting Line buying shoes, as we do at least twice a year, and we
find that we are quite taken with our shoe salesman. It is hard
not to fall in love with a really well-trained, highly motivated,
very attentive shoe salesman, is it not? I mean, he's on his
knees in front of you, caressing your feet and paying attention;
we can ask little else from a man. Naturally, we fell to fawning
over him and praising him to the skies, which only served to
increase his fervor for our feet and the shoes in which to
enshrine them. Oh, it was a happy, happy circle we had going.

By and by, during this shoe purchase/courtship, Tammy
asked our young man his name, to which he replied, "Adam."
A momentary silence ensued. "Mind if we call you Bob?" I
asked. He graciously, speedily, and without question replied,
"Why no, of course not, please do." This just pushed us right

over the cliff in love with him on the spot. Here was a guy happily willing to do whatever it took to please us. So fear not if there is a dearth of Bobs in your home area: A willing attitude makes up for a lot.

No Humans Harmed in This Research

Quite a few great analogous stories from the animal kingdom have been reported to me. Occasionally I will read something for myself and remember a fair number of details; more often, however, somebody else will read something interesting and tell me about it, and of that, I will remember the parts I personally find entertaining. Whether or not they are founded in fact is completely immaterial to me, as I imagine it is to you as well; otherwise, you'd be reading *Scientific American* instead of this book. No animals have told me any of the stories discussed herein. Animals don't talk to me directly, although a cat we had once willed me telepathically to name her Debbie. Otis, the brown dog who lives with my nephew, Trevor Palmer, in New Orleans and sometimes with his mother, my sister, Judy, does talk to Judy occasionally. He very softly says "Wow" when he is particularly moved about something, usually the prospect of eating a plateful of pink weenies up in the middle of Judy's bed. Otis loves them pink weenies, and he does love to eat in bed.

No, It's a Hole in the Head We Don't Need

At any rate, I heard a story about a bird. I'm pretty sure Martha Thomas told me about it. Martha has a genius IQ, is always reading and remembering and telling me what she reads. Being the one-trick pony that I am, I make a joke out of the stuff. Anyway, I think it was the Alaskan snowy owl, but I could be wrong, so if you're a bird fanatic, don't get all in a wad. The story is what's important, and if we are attributing a characteristic to the Alaskan snowy owl that belongs to some other bird, what possible difference does it make? Don't tell them, and they won't care.

It seems that the female Alaskan snowy owl will not acknowledge the existence of the male Alaskan snowy owl until such time as he presents her with a dead mouse. Not just any ole dead mouse—it can't be one he just had lying around that maybe some other, very picky, girl owl rejected. It must be an extremely fresh dead mouse, and it must be of the appropriate size as to demonstrate clearly the degree of esteem in which he holds her, the object of his affection. He may bring dead mice for days and weeks and she will, of course, eat them right up. She will just eat and ignore him. Until the perfect mouse is presented—the, say, three-to-four-carat mouse—she will not acknowledge to her suitor that the mouse came from him. He is, by this time, wild with desire—and only for her. Doesn't he give up and write her off, taking his dead mice to a more receptive girl owl? Oh no. He becomes completely transfixed by her. He is driven to please her and only her with his mouse prowess. If he goes without getting laid for a month of Sundays, he will persist in hauling dead mice for her perusal/consumption, clinging blindly to the hope and belief that he will prevail.

Now, the story told to me did not include any suggestion that the girl Alaskan snowy owl might ever be so mindless as to just give it up for a substandard mouse, or worse, for gratis, or worst of all, just to make him happy. But we don't have to stretch our imaginations too far to get a picture of it, do we? I, for one, have started demanding to see some dead mice around here, and right quick, too. My current fiancé lives two hundred miles away—which makes me like him just a whole lot more—and he has to run up and down the highway all the time just to see me. He seems happy to do so. This is the appropriate attitude for a fiancé, certainly. I shared the dead mouse story with him, and he caught on to it right quick. "You want jewelry, don't you?" he asked, in a not-unpleasant tone— in fact, he actually seemed pretty jovial about it. I sighed, and said, Yes, I suppose I do—just no solitaires at this point unless they are on a chain, and don't be eyeing my left hand, either, buckwheat. I've just gotten him broken in good as a fiancé, I ain't messing up this deal any time soon, thank you.

He wanted some help in picking out the right dead mouse, and I was more than willing to give it to him. He said men hate buying gifts for women because they always get the wrong thing, and even though we make a fuss over it, they can tell we hate it. So what I do, and what I advise all of you to do as well, is cultivate a relationship with a good jeweler—one who will write down what you like and keep it handy in case anybody comes in asking. Of course, your best friend should look out for you as well. When my best buddy, Allison Church, was celebrating the tenth anniversary of her marriage to the gift-igmo David, I took matters and him in hand and had the most fabulous ring in the history of the world made for her. David was overjoyed to give her something she so obviously loved. He was less than thrilled about paying for it, but hey, he got over it.

I think we should get together regularly with our girl-friends and talk about what kinds of dead mice we'd like and everybody pick somebody else's boyfriend, fiancé, or husband—maybe draw names—and advise them. Call it a Dead Mouse Party and make all your favorite Sweet Potato Queens' party foods and beverages. This is as good an occasion for a party as I personally have ever heard.

About the same time I was doing all that heavy thinking about snowy owls and mice, I was also reading that "Mars and Venus" stuff about men and women. I hate to say it, but that John Gray guy makes sense. He includes at least twenty-five conversations that I personally have had with assorted men over the years—I'm talking word for word practically. Anyway, John Gray says that many problems in relationships are caused by women doing too much for guys. When they like us and we like them, we naturally want to do more and more stuff for them and be sweet to them. What could be wrong with that? Well, it just doesn't work—that is all. They hate it when we do that. This totally supports the theory advanced in *SPQBOL*: Treat 'Em Like Shit and Never Give 'Em Any and They'll Follow You Around Like Dogs. And I think John Gray was saying exactly that, too, only with more genteel language. And then this snowy owl business comes up. In that particular study, there was no mention of a girl snowy owl ever bringing a dead mouse to a boy snowy owl—not once, not ever in the history of snowy owls. Those snowy owl bitches have figured out the deal and they are sticking with what works.

Now, it would seem that creatures with penises are highly likely to be hardwired with a need to please creatures without penises. And since they only value what they have to work hard to get, we should cease and desist doing anything nice to attract them. It goes against their nature. Instead, we should allow them to bring us presents, but we should not be entirely satisfied with any of them, so that they can work harder at pleasing us in the future. To make them completely happy, we must reject a certain number of their offerings to provide them with even more opportunities for pleasing us.

I think I'm getting the hang of the scientific method.